JOY 123

Jesus First
Others Second
You Third

GD Dowey

RIGHTEOUS ACTS PUBLISHING

ISBN 978-1-7359876-2-0
Library of Congress Control Number: 2021907908

Righteous Acts Publishing
Irmo, South Carolina

In loving memory of Bunny, [Eunice Stockman Dowey, my grandmother], who prayed for me and took me to church and revival meetings, and gave me my first Bible. She was the embodiment of love and peace and joy in my life. She was patient on God, and lived her life by faith in Him. She was happy in Christ on this planet for 85 years...these days she is joyful in Him for eternity in heaven.

Table of Contents

Preface

From some of my earliest recollections of youth group at church our student minister preached and taught the elementary, acronymic phrase, *JOY·123*. Decoded, it means, "Jesus first, Others second, and You and me third." It was foundational in our young catechismal training as we learned to be true disciples in Christ. As I began editing this little study on Paul's great work of Philippians, I searched for the title, any title, of any work for "JOY·123," and I found none. "It can't be" I said to myself. There need to be more books written on enjoying the Christian life by simplistic, easy to remember acronyms of creeds. They cause us to be constantly reminded to put Christ first.

We need simple books of dogma directing us on primarily choosing Christ, putting others ahead of ourselves, humbly bowing to Jesus, and dying to our selfish sin. How can we grow up to maturity in joyful living if we don't have basic introductions of putting Jesus first, our neighbors and enemies second, and ourselves last? What does putting Jesus first even mean? Do we really put the needs of others ahead of ourselves? Is it possible to live in a world where we live out Christ's claim to be servants, rather than to be served? Despite our misgivings, JOY·123 is the way He has commanded us to live this life.

Here's the caveat: It's a mean world for the Christ follower. It's filled with suffering and persecution for the true believer. Rejection and hurt are commonplace for the man, woman, and child who take up their cross to follow Jesus. So we are desperate for Holy Spirit-led awakenings to how to live expectant on His joy. Our hope for real joy is in Him only. As G.K. Chesterton said, "God is the happiest being in the universe."

Our God is well acquainted with burden. Isaiah said,

> *"He was despised and rejected by men, a man of sorrows and acquainted with grief; and as one from whom men hide their faces he was despised, and we esteemed him not."*   *-Isaiah 53:3*

Yet He burgeons with joy and happiness. Understand that God's wrath is of His justice, His sorrow, and His mercy in response to a fallen world. In His holiness, this world will be made right and the world's pain and sorrow will be banished one day. God's basic characteristic is joy. He has to be the happiest being in the universe, and He is. Joy is the attitude and feeling of the treasure found in the saving grace of Christ Jesus.

'How do people live without true joy?' I asked myself. Incredibly, the Bible devotes an entire book to delineating the subject of joy in Christ. It's called the book of Philippians. In only four short chapters, we see something portrayed that is entirely foreign to our American culture of habitually collecting the most toys. Joy is not found in exotic vacations, wardrobe changes, or the latest mobile device. Rather, joy is only found in bowing to King Jesus. Remarkably, joy is only mentioned five times in Paul's joy-infested letter. However, Paul states verbatim: You and I need to practice the bow because one day everyone will bow, regardless. The bow brings joy.

Joy comes from the Greek word, χαρας (charás) and it does mean joy, but there is an attachment. It's joy that is in us because of His grace. We get the English word *charisma,* or *charismatic,* from the Koinonia Greek. There is a demonstrative feeling from these words. Χαρας is a response to God! Therefore, joy is not something you can buy at the mall or off of Amazon. Joy is somewhat of a by-product of God's grace in you and your acknowledgment to Him for His goodness and salvation in Christ. Succinctly put, we have joy because of God's gift, not because we have learned to entertain ourselves, put a smile on our faces, and make ourselves jolly.

This does not mean we can give up our search for joy and sit back and hope it just happens our way. No, joy is a fruit of discipline and of seeking Him. It should describe your life for now and eternity. The great C.S. Lewis said, "Joy is the serious business of heaven." So we must keep looking, keep digging, keep seeking, keep knocking, and, for the sake of God's glory, keep reading His Holy Word to discover true joy.

To a large extent, joy is a learning experience. If I reflect on my toddler years in church, it's one of the first things those saintly ladies were teaching us as they taught us to sing, "I've got the joy, joy, joy, joy down in my heart (where?). Down in my heart, down in my heart. I've got the joy, joy, joy, joy down in my heart to stay." Oh my, what a lesson this world needs...a lesson in joy where Jesus comes into your heart...a lesson where even a four-year-old can repeat it.

Chapter 1

Starting Again

Paul and Timothy, servants of Christ Jesus,
To all the saints in Christ Jesus who are at
Philippi, with the overseers and deacons:
Grace to you and peace from God our
Father and the Lord Jesus Christ.
I thank my God in all my remembrance of
you, always in every prayer of mine for you
all making my prayer with joy, because of
your partnership in the gospel from the
first day until now. And I am sure of this,
that he who began a good work in you will
bring it to completion at the day of Jesus
Christ.

*   -Philippians 1:1-6*

Have you ever started something that you haven't finished? I have, plenty of times, and I regretted it. And there have been many times where I started something years back, let it go, then recovered a desire and got up enough gumption to finish it. It was an exhilarating feeling. That sense of accomplishment at a project's completion is difficult to beat. I can look back and see plenty of things I bemoan ever beginning, and plenty more I wish I could go back and finish. But for most things it's hopelessly, and honestly, too late.

It's never too late to start a relationship with God or to continue. Philippians is that book that encourages us to finish what we committed to, and to complete our calling in Christ Jesus. It is a letter sent to the church at Philippi, the first church started by Paul in Southeast Europe— in Greece. Paul's first convert there was Lydia, a woman who sold purple goods. Women had a prominent role in the church at Philippi, a fact worth noting.

The short, four-chapter book describes the pleasurable life in Christ. It echoes the Psalter's words,

Delight yourself in the Lord, and He
will give you the desires of your heart.
                                        -Psalm 37:4

Despite the conditions for his writing (Paul was in jail as he wrote), the theme of Philippians is joy. Yes, joy. How can that be? Paul was suffering in prison. You can bet it wasn't a cot and three warm meals a day. There was no recreation and TV time. It was a difficult period for the church and the people of God. However, there was the genuine living of joy. The modern day, universal definition of joy usually involves worldly leisure, surplus stuff, and mo' money. But in Philippians Paul is talking about real, true joy. It can be difficult for us to understand this joy found in the Bible, since they were devoid of twenty-first century technology, travel, and communication.

That's just it— somewhere along the way we've received bad information about living the Christian life. We have equated being a successful Christian with money, riches, entertainment, and hedonistic living. Contemporary preaching parallels it with the American dream. As it's portrayed in our society— especially in the modern-day secular church (if that is such a thing)— unless you are

2

overly educated, bountifully employed, immensely wealthy, extravagantly dressed, and extremely impressed, then you are a sad person.

In this opening chapter, in a very short time, we are going to size up our living. If you don't have real joy in your life in Christ— I'm not saying your life will end this year— but if you keep going the route of continual sadness, then your life is getting shorter and sourer as it moves quicker.

You desperately need to see and live out the book of Philippians in your life. Because in this new progressive world order of rapid downward spiraling— in other words, *sin*— you sincerely need to know what real joy is.

Joy is a by-product, a fruit, more so than it is an emotion. Joy is simply implementing the biblical principle of the Great Commandment which is found in Matthew 22:37,38. When we put God first in our lives and our neighbor second, somehow God makes it into joy for us. Plant God's seed in your life and He guarantees the produce of joyful fruit!

I like to say it the way I titled this book: J·O·Y·1·2·3. Jesus – first, Others second, You (me) third. It's elementary. It's only three moves. It is easy to remember. When you come to a dead end in your life or your life is stalled, then the answer is always J·O·Y·1·2·3. If your livelihood is stalled then live by J·O·Y·1·2·3 and things will turn around quickly, I promise.

Motivational seminars and books pertaining to success inundate our world. The idea from those achievement authors and sensation pushers is that you just need to *start*. They ask, "Do you want to retire early and wealthy? Start!" At the start of every new year, we are encouraged to lose weight. How? Just start exercising, they say. Start dieting, they say. Need a job? Start looking, they say. Want to read 40 books this year, they say, you have to start somewhere. A lot of people want to run half-marathons but starting them is not the problem, it's finishing. I can attest personally from last year's 13.1-miler. I got twelve miles into it and everything in my body just wanted to quit. I wouldn't let it. They said, "Quit" and I told myself I had to finish. It is definitely a mind-over-matter story. You can start an education, you can start healthy living and eating, you can start a marriage, you can start a family, you can start on retirement, and you can get in the starting crouch in a 440 or an 880, but the real dilemma is, how do you finish?

I know this guy who was morbidly obese and one day he just decided to quit eating to lose weight. I guess, in his mind, it worked for about a day. But he soon got sick because there was no plan to lose the 175 pounds he planned on shedding. After being sick for two weeks because he hadn't eaten, he finally began educating himself on how to lose the weight in a healthy way. And he did it! He finished. He got down to his optimum weight. Now he consults, writes, and encourages others to do the same. Anyone can start anything. Starting has proved to be no problem for most people, but it's getting to that finish line that seems to be the big deal, and that involves discipline.

Before we look at the right way to finish well, and to finish the race of life, let me point out something to you here. Paul says,

> And I am sure of this, <u>that he who began</u> a good work in you will bring it to completion at the day of Jesus Christ.
> -Philippians 1:6

Notice something: it's not *you* who began the good work, it's He, who began it *in* you. What is the good work? It is your transformation. It's the change in your life. Joy comes after the change. For the life of me I don't get why we don't comprehend that the Christian life is about you changing every day. Most people want to repeat that oft-used line, "I don't like change!" If you are a Christ-follower, then you have committed to change, and to keep changing to become more like Him. As you change you are moving toward real joy. The Christian life means never staying the same, but constantly changing. You must change. You have to change to become more like Christ.

You cannot expect to grow in grace if you don't read the Scriptures.
- Charles Spurgeon

Nothing will change your life like the Word of God. Absolutely nothing. I wrote down the other day, in the leaves of my note-taking Bible, these words: "If you want to grow to understand the Gospel, then you must see it on every page in the Bible." Yes, when you can look at every story, every principle, every statute, every time God made a covenant with the people and they broke it...whenever you can look at the pages and people and see that you and I are grossly inept, woefully short of living right, terribly sinful, that we miss the bullseye and blatantly disobey God, and that our only hope is God stepping in and providing for us...whenever you can see that on every page, whenever you can identify with those men and women of old, *then* you are on the right track of understanding God more and knowing joy.

The more reverence we have for the Word of God, the more joy we shall find in it. *-Matthew Henry*

If you are trying to be happy by living the phrase, "God helps those who help themselves," then I've got bad news for you. Jesus came to us because we could not go to Him. Jesus helps us because we are unable to help ourselves. Jesus gives us joy because without Him joy does not exist.

5

God changes you from loser to winner if you are a Christ-follower. He began the change in your life. He justified you. That means He saved you. He rescued you. It's not you who did it. It's not you who started it. He did it. I didn't say it, Scripture does. He called you, He saw you and He chose you out of His love. Go all the way back in the Old Testament to Genesis 12. The scene isn't that one day Abraham was kicking a can down the road and thinking about following God. No, the Bible says God called on Abraham and told him to get up, and pack up, and go to where He would tell him. Abraham was a reprobate, and not a fearer of God. He was hopeless before God called him. He had no chance for joy.

You see, if you are a Christ follower and you messed up, and if you have openly rebelled against the Creator, and if you have decidedly and purposefully flipped Him off inside your head because you were hurt by something inside your heart, or if you decided you would take a break last year, the year before, and the year before that, and for some reason you find yourself in God's presence this year— maybe at church, maybe not— maybe with the fellowship of other believers, maybe not— I have great, tremendous news for you! God considers you still in the ballgame. In other words, God is not finished with you yet.

So, the question is, *how do I start again,* and then finish well? The answer to that is the key to discovering joy.

1. Start being a servant again

Ten years ago, I went to see Robert Plant and the *Band of Joy* in concert. Led Zeppelin fans know the all-time great, golden-maned, rock 'n roll front man. His latest collection of artists and instrumentalists (he has had several over the years) were known as the Band of Joy. As I sat waiting for the music to begin, I looked up at the colorful curtain sign advertising the band and said, "That's the church." We should be a band of joy! Joy in your life and mine and in the church comes from serving on the stage of life.

The letter of Philippians starts with Paul identifying himself and Timothy as precisely who they were. Not bigshots, not super-saints, not powerful religious types, but servants. They didn't have the big head.

> *Most of us go through life worrying people will think too little of us. Paul worried people would think too much of him.*   *-D.A. Horton*

Way too many people get involved in church work for the payday, for the Christian Academy Awards, or for just simple every week approval. Read Scripture from beginning to finish and you will find servanthood is as essential to the Christian as water is to a fish. The beauty of serving is that you can start anytime and people won't know that you haven't been doing it all your life! If anyone had the resumé to float out there in order to elevate himself to a certain spiritual superior status, then it would have been the Apostle Paul. Yet he declares his servant standing over and over. In one translation Paul refers to himself as a slave to Christ.

Your Christian life, and your joy in living it, depends on your service to the King. Seek Him by studying the Word of God and by finding the place where He is calling you to serve Him. Then pour everything into that, and you will discover what real joy is all about. Quit looking for the feeling before you look to serve. Start serving, and the feelings of joy will naturally flow. Where do you start serving? First, by serving God. Second, by serving and loving others. Third, well, you are last. The good news is Jesus says the last will be first!

2. Start praying again

Paul starts the letter with his own praise report, saying he thanks God and that he remembers the people, the church at Philippi, in prayer. You need to start praying again. People usually begin each new year by writing down their resolutions and promises. Believe me, the economy banks on people who are full of starts, especially in the area of weight loss and nutrition. But our question is, who will finish the year seeking God?

Missie and I read through the Bible every year. Every year. Interestingly, it was close for me last year! I finished on New Year's Eve. It was fantastic. What I started, I finished. Nothing in life will be as rewarding and gratifying as when we commit to reading the Word of God each year, and finish. Do it, I beg you, it's one of the most spiritually gratifying disciplines you can do.

Each year starts full-force, and you never know what is coming. I am reminded that I didn't pray enough last year. I didn't. I could give you a number that measures my hours spent on my knees, but it was not enough. I have to pray more this year. I often feel a little like Oscar Schindler, in the movie *Schindler's List,* when he lamented over the fact that he could have sold something else, to raise more money to save more Jews from the Nazi gas chambers. I could have prayed more last year. Would it have meant that one more person would have come to Christ and escaped eternal death? It's very possible. As a Christ-follower who wants to glorify God and grow closer to Him, He calls you to pray more. I have to grow closer to Him this year if I am going to make it in this life. If I am going to have joy, then I need to pray for others. It's amazing how that works. I pray for the spiritual and physical health of others and for God to richly bless them, and I receive joy. It may sound strange, but I experience it constantly.

All of us would be wiser if we would resolve never to put people down, except on our prayer list.

-D.A. Carson

Joy originates from our time with God. There is almost nothing left for me to say, except this:

3. Start to understand that God started it, and God will finish it!

Don't miss the key to Philippians— *joy.* It goes by so fast in the first six verses of this chapter that you may have missed it. Paul says: *when I pray for you, I pray with joy.* That is so good I had to go back and check it again myself. It's true! He begins this letter to the church at Philippi by telling them he prays for them with a smile of remembrance in his heart, happiness for their partnership in growth, and elated anticipation for the future. All of this equals joy.

Joy is vital to the Christ follower. As difficult as it is to live the Christian life, as hard as it is to suffer for Christ, as massive as it is to know your pain in Christ serves to shape you into His man or woman, you have to have some joy. And you need to recognize the joy. Joy is not merely a feeling. Some preachers would say it's not a feeling at all. Instead, joy is realizing God is in control. If God is not sovereign, totally in control, then God is not God. There is joy in knowing His power despite your hurting circumstances. There is joy in knowing that you are safe no matter the perils of life.

We first encounter Philippi in Acts. It's the second missionary journey, Paul and Silas are joined by Timothy, and they find themselves in Greece in an important trade city called Philippi. A church is started, and Paul shares the Gospel with Lydia. Lydia, remember, deals in purple stuff. Folks in the psychedelic age of the 1960's would have sought her out for her stylish cloth. An important event in Acts is when Lydia put her faith and trust in Jesus.

The story gets interesting. Paul is doing exactly what He was called to do. He was faithful, and he starts a church. He leads a prominent woman to Christ, and there is certainly happiness and joy that results from the fruit of obedience, but then... *BAM!* A fortune-teller, of all things, gets in Paul's face and starts putting down the Gospel. Paul gets tired of her and he simply casts out the demon from her. When the demon came out, out went her ability to tell the future— or the past, or fortune, or whatever. What Paul didn't know— or if he did, he didn't care— was that the fortune-teller was being pimped out by a pimp. And these hustlers, the woman's "owners," raised so much ruckus over what Paul did that Paul and Silas were thrown in jail.

Here's the part you need to get, but first let me ask you: What would you be doing at midnight in jail? Sleeping? Trying to protect yourself? Crying? Begging for mercy? Complaining? Blaming someone else? Blaming God? Looking for a way out? Beating yourself up for getting into this mess? That is not at all what Paul and Silas were doing.

> *About midnight Paul and Silas were praying and singing hymns to God, and the prisoners were listening to them, and suddenly there was a great earthquake, so that the foundations of the prison were shaken. And immediately all the doors were opened, and everyone's bonds were unfastened.*   *-Acts 16:25,26*

Pay attention to this spiritual fact: **Sin is the thief of joy**. No one else steals your joy. You give it away when you reject God and eject God out of your life. Your joy, my joy, is tied directly to our understanding of our relationship to God and not to our circumstances. There was no worse place to be in all the world than in a Turkish-style prison, hanging in chains after you have been beaten. But to Paul and Silas it was the most joyful place in all the world. How can that be? Because they were with God and that is all the source you need for pure joy.

There was a cowboy who went to buy some life insurance. The broker asked him if he had any accidents in the past year, to which the cowboy replied, "No. But I was kicked by a mule, stepped on by a raging bull, chased by hyena, and bitten by a rattlesnake – all that laid me up for a while."

The agent jumped up and said, "Weren't they accidents?"

The cowboy said, "No, they did it on purpose."

The cowboy realized something that you and I badly need to realize: there are no such things as true accidents. The enemy is against us and resolves to destroy us. The good news is that God is for us.

Everything that happens to you and me is known by our great God. For those who are in Christ, you may think that you started it, but you didn't. He did. He is the one that called you. He knew His men were hanging by their arms in chains in prison, and He also knows the difficulty you are going through today. Maybe you think you are in prison? It could be that you are. A prison of doubt, guilt, or shame; a personal jail cell of meaninglessness, and a life without purpose that you are beating yourself up over. You may think that being sidelined last year, or for the past two years, or ten years, was all because you said, "I'm going to interrupt God's plan for my life and take a vacation." Nope, what He starts, He finishes.

*And I am sure of this, that **he who** began a good work in you will bring it to*

completion at the day of Jesus Christ.
                              -Philippians 1:6

It's not Yoo-hoo. It's not Boo-Hoo. It's not Cindy-Lou Who. It's **He who**. *He who started it is going to finish it.* Do you know why? God is not like you and me. We conduct experiments, God carries out a plan. We are scientific, He is creative and the Creator. We do things partially. God does things in completion. It's *He who*, not you who.

Look at all the examples of *He who* in the New Testament:

> *Where is **he who** has been born king of the Jews? For we saw his star when it rose and have come to worship him.*
>   *-Matthew 2:2*

> *I baptize you with water for repentance, but **he who** is coming after me is mightier than I.*   *-Matthew 3:1*

> *And **he who** searches hearts   knows what is the mind of the Spirit, because the Spirit intercedes for the saints according to the will of God.*   *-Romans 8:27*

> ***He who** did not spare his own Son but gave him up for us all, how will he not also with him graciously give us all things?*
>   *-Romans 8:32*

All of our Hee-Haw attempts at living this life, trying to find happiness, security, and comfort, is causing us to quit, to come up short, and to avoid the finish. Don't blame God or anyone else for you not being joyful. If you are sad and lonely, it's because you have given your joy away. You've quit on God, even though He never quits on you. You have allowed the circumstances in your life to dictate how you feel instead of believing God's promises. You have let sin win, when you didn't have to. I don't think He's calling you to finish your life today. Maybe He is, however, *He who began a good work in you....*

Consider what Paul says: I am confident, I am sure, I *know*, that He who began that good work is going to take it on to a great finish. He is for sure calling you to start serving, start praying, and to start moving on with God. And when you do, it is going to be a fantastic finish, and you will certainly find joy.

Chapter 1 – **JOY123** Study Guide:

01 List some ways you can serve **JESUS** practically in your neighborhood. Here are some that are guaranteed to bring a surreptitious joy:

- ⮑ Have you ever invited your neighbor to church?
- ⮑ In a time of crisis, you have a perfect opportunity to pray and lead others in prayer.
- ⮑ Give Bibles as gifts, they always spark conversation about the Savior.
- ⮑ Do these things and you will begin to experience joy.

02 Write down in one sentence how you felt after you gave your time to give to **OTHERS**:

_____

_____

Y3 If **YOU** are not praying, it's easy to start. Write out three prayer requests and pray for five minutes each day, for one week. Record how you feel at the end of the week toward those requests. Prayer is not for God, it's for you!

Facts about prayer:
- ➲ Once you start, before too long you realize you need more time
- ➲ Once you commit more time to prayer, the more the enemy will attack you for it
- ➲ Once you begin being attacked, you will cry out to Him more
- ➲ That's where God wants you to be

Your 3 Prayer Requests:

➲

➲

➲

Chapter 2

What's Your Hurry?

For to me to live is Christ, and to die is gain. If I am to live in the flesh, that means fruitful labor for me. Yet which I shall choose I cannot tell. I am hard pressed between the two. My desire is to depart and be with Christ, for that is far better. But to remain in the flesh is more necessary on your account. Convinced of this, I know that I will remain and continue with you all, for your progress and joy in the faith, so that in me you may have ample cause to glory in Christ Jesus, because of my coming to you again.

-Philippians 1:21-26

What is there to live for? You have to live for joy, period. Without joy, life is not worth living. Jesus is joy. Is He *your* joy?

There is a famous scene in *The Shawshank Redemption* where Andy is talking to Red, dreaming about one day getting out. He is envisioning Zihuantanejo, Mexico, and going there to spend the rest of his life on a fishing boat

15

in the Pacific. Red is pessimistic and thinks Andy is torturing himself with that dream to get out of prison, because Andy is in for life. But as they lean against a stone wall, talking, Andy remains adamant about sticking to his wish and goal. He says to Red, "You got to get busy living or get busy dying."

Get busy living or get busy dying— what a quote! Before Jesus came into the world, those were your only options, and they amounted to the same thing. To live heartedly and to die miserably. You may be lucky enough to live on the Pacific coastline downing coffee shots and eating avocado toast, but what do you do after that? It really defines our culture doesn't it? People are trying to learn to live better, to accumulate more, to relax greatly, to live longer, and to be as happy as we can be despite the circumstances. Then there is the other option: to die poor, to fade away quietly, to deteriorate and decline as gracefully as possible while suffering as little as possible. Both end up in the same place for those without Christ. I've checked it out, and life does not last much past 75-80 years. We've fooled ourselves. The Puritan preacher Jonathan Edwards said, "Have I allowed myself to become blinded by the deceitful nature of habitually gratified sin?" Either way, we get busy living or we get busy dying. That's it. And either way we end up the same: separated from God.

For thousands of years, that was the approach. But oh, how things changed when Jesus came into this pathetic world. But, sadly, over the next two thousand years many ignored the new way of life and stuck with the old paradigm of two choices— living and dying. It's natural in this world. When we look at the world from our natural state, that's what we are left with— living and dying. It's tragic. And, even more tragically, millions today believe they are living when they are actually dying. Their approach is that old, "let's find the fountain of youth" type of mentality. How's it going for you?

I love healthy eating and living. I feel a lot better when I eat correctly and get plenty of exercise. I experience more aches and pains when I don't. But how long will good eating and jogging really sustain me? Has anyone ever met a faith healer who lived to be a hundred? The Bible says it: "no one will live beyond 120 years." And guess what? No one has. Nor have I ever met anyone who wants to get old and spend their last years, forgotten, in a nursing home.

Get busy living or get busy dying sounds good for motivational purposes. And it's a fantastic rallying cry if you are down in the dumps and need a one-liner that will get you to refocus your attention on the important things. *Get busy living or get busy dying* is a tremendous line if all of your truth is based on Hollywood movies or New York Times bestsellers. But this is real life. And our magnificent God did not graciously invade this planet with some of the same old answers that you can get on any street corner or purchase for $1.99 in paperback on Amazon. No, He has something better. You can get busy living, you can get busy dying, or you can get busy with Jesus. Maybe better put: *get busy dying to yourself and living for Jesus*. Joy is experienced when we engage in relationship with Christ. That is exactly what the end of chapter 1 in Philippians says. Once more:

> *For to me to live is Christ, and to die is gain.* If I am to live in the flesh, that means fruitful labor for me. Yet which I shall choose I cannot tell. I am hard pressed between the two. My desire is to depart and be with Christ, for that is far better. But to remain in the flesh is more necessary on your account. Convinced of this, I know that I will remain and continue with you all, for your progress and joy in the faith, so that in me you may have ample cause to glory in Christ Jesus, because of

Every time you hear the word *Philippians*, remember to associate it with **joy**. I picture it as that delightful little church that the Apostle Paul was sent to in that coastal city near the Aegean Sea. And he states joyous living succinctly in this section. It is living for Christ. Philippians is important because this was the first church started in Europe. Paul calls our attention to the third choice in life, which is getting busy with Jesus. You have three choices. Look at the options, and when we conclude this chapter, my prayer is that you will be able to identify where you stand. But let me tell you something: you have to pick one of the three. Getting busy— getting on with it— and doing something with your life is massive.

Don't go through this life, arriving at the end, and all you have to show for it is for them to have a little church service or bar party where they eat potato salad or raise a whiskey glass in your name. Avoid having your obituary read, "She liked to do crossword puzzles and water her flowers." Make sure it doesn't say, "He was a Detroit Lions fan and loved macaroni and cheese." Please avoid (this one is fresh, I read it this morning), "He enjoyed the Gamecocks, the Braves, and his Chevrolet trucks. He liked doing his yard work and had many flowers." Folks, there's more to it than just busy living and busy dying. Here's the direction we should go:

1. Stop the Busy Living!

There are all kinds of busy living. There is busy-work living, there is busy-entertainment living, there is busy-body living, and there is busy-money-making living. To tell the truth, we are just too busy. What is your greatest spiritual challenge? Before you think that it's not going to church enough, or not loving your neighbor, I want to stop

18

you in your tracks and give you the answer: *The greatest challenge to our spiritual lives is we press the accelerator too hard.* Speed kills, and so does driving 155mph constantly. We are getting killed all day long if we are not walking with Jesus. What's that mean, *killed?* It means your spiritual life is being murdered and you can't even see it until it's too late. In a world where we think we have to go fast to succeed, Jesus slows us down for real success. Solve this one problem and everything else is solved in your life with God. Everything! Here it is...

Your greatest spiritual challenge is -H-U-R-R-Y-

"Greg, why do you think this is the problem in my life?" Because you won't admit it.

A friend of a friend, Pastor Wang Yi, got nine years of hard time in a Chinese prison not too long ago. They arrested him without much fanfare. The reason? Preaching in the street.

First let me explain to you how Satan, the enemy, does *not* operate. Traditional cliché has him showing up in a Chinese Church with a pitchfork, in a red-hooded suit, with Black Sabbath playing in the background and he yells some expletives with, "I'm going to shut this church down!" All the while making maniacal demonic faces. No, he doesn't operate like that.

He instead has someone leaning his way, employed in downtown government, who convinces the local authorities that the church building would be a great museum for the new Chinese exhibit. Using this approach, by a few strokes of a pen and several armed guards, they take down the red cross, found on the top of every legal Chinese Church, and then kick the church out of town. Another approach may be to raise their taxes. All the Asian brothers and sisters have to do is to give hundreds of thousands of dollars in taxes and they can stay. The Chinese church is not like the rich American ministries you see on television. The church can't pay, are deemed an obstruction of justice, and the doors are shuttered.

We are far more likely to run into Satan by using our mobile phones than we are to find him lurking in some desolate back alley of our lives. Yes, that time when you are reading your Bible for the day and you get an alert on your phone causing you to refocus your attention to something else. I'm not saying the devil controls the microwaves and soundwaves, triggering an alert on your phone. What I am saying is you and I are so afraid we are going to miss something that we refuse to totally give God our time, thinking we can manage several gods at once.

> *If the devil can't make you sin, he will make you busy.*
>> *-Corrie Ten Boom*

Carl Jung the famous German psychologist said:

> *Hurry is not of the devil, it is the devil.*

Every day someone will ask me, "How are you doing?" Most likely my response will be, "I'm fine – just busy." Pay attention and you will find this true on all fronts, across social class, ethnicity, between males and females. College students are busy, young parents are busy, empty-nesters are busy, retirees living on the golf course are busy, CEOs are busy. So are baristas and nannies, grandpas and grand-mammies. Americans are busy, Germans are busy, and Russians are busy. My goodness, read the New Testament and you will find that Jesus was busy! The problem isn't that you have too much to do, it's that you have a lot to do and the only way to keep the plates spinning and the balls

20

juggling is to hurry. Jesus was busy, but examine the New Testament and you see He was never rushed.

A professor in a Southern university conducted a study and found the obstacles to Christian growth. He surveyed over 20,000 Christians, and found out that busyness was the number one distraction from spiritual life. Here's what he concluded:

⮞ Christians are adapting to a culture of busyness, hurry and overload
which leads to...
⮞ God becoming more marginalized in Christians' lives
which leads to...
⮞ a diminishing relationship with God
which leads to...
⮞ Christians becoming even more vulnerable to adopting secular assumptions about how to live
which leads to...
⮞ more conformity to a culture of busyness, hurry and overload.

And then the cycle begins again.

And let me tell you, pastors are the worst. Every week, there is a story of burnout, often on a high level, in the pastorate. I work on it all of the time— to not get in a hurry. Hurry, as a pastor, leads to too many bad things: you begin worrying about more money, a bigger building, more staff, and more achievement. Hurry leads to thinking *you* have to do something for God instead of allowing God to work through you. Hurry is a joy zapper! A hurried soul cannot live effectively for the Lord. Hurry leads to us doing, rather than just being for the Lord Jesus.

We usually talk about our walk with Jesus, not our run. Hurry is the death of prayer. Hurry is the enemy of Bible study and reading. Hurry is the complete opposite of how our great God wants us to live. There is nothing that is done in a hurry that can't be better done without it. Yes, a certain amount of busyness makes sense, especially if your wife's water breaks or if there is a fire, but 9-1-1 living for the Christian is criminal. If 9-1-1 for God is on your speed dial, then take it off. Hurry is for the Good News announcement, not Good News living. Preach and teach Jesus with a sense of urgency, live the Christian life like you are walking in the park. And for the sake of the church, make sure your pastor gets time off!

It's not just our emotional health that is at risk and reaching a point of no return. Our spiritual health is suffering the most. And most of us want to solve it with a quick call or text to God about how we can be happy this week, hoping He doesn't answer so we can put off that talk until next time. And we add, "...make sure, God, that it's only a sentence or two, I hate long texts."

Our world has sped up to a frenetic pace. We feel it in our bones and we surely feel it on the interstate as we put the pedal to the metal. It hasn't always been this way. Roman playwright, Plautus got angry about the invention of the sun dial! Look what he wrote:

The gods confound the man who first found out
How to distinguish hours! Confound him, too,
Who in this place set up a sun-dial
To cut and hack my days so wretchedly
Into small portions!

And then the clock, and then the watch, and what do you know? Along comes 2007, and Steve Jobs gave us the iPhone, and a few months later came Facebook and, the same year, Twitter, and then the App store. I would love to hear what Plautus would say about the Apple Watch where we can get calls, texts, and emails on our wrists. The rest is an awful history, and this hurry-up attitude and lifestyle is just murdering us. Here are ten symptoms of hurry sickness:

- ⮞ Irritability
- ⮞ Hypersensitivity
- ⮞ Restlessness
- ⮞ Workaholism
- ⮞ Emotional Numbness
- ⮞ Out-of-order priorities
- ⮞ Lack of care for your body
- ⮞ Escapist behaviors
- ⮞ Slippage of spiritual disciplines
- ⮞ Isolation

Here's the deal: an over-busy, overloaded, hurried-lifestyle speed is the new norm, and it's toxic! Thirty-nine percent of Americans are more anxious than they were a year ago. Hurry is killing us spiritually, and it also kills relationships. Love takes time, hurry doesn't have it— and hurry just points to a disordered heart.

What is the solution? They are not manufacturing more hours for your day or days for your week. Should you volunteer more? Should you take up a hobby or workout? That just requires more time. Your solution to your busyness is not to add, but to slow down. What should you do?

-Slow down, live your life around that which counts-

2. Get Busy Dying...to yourself

The things I have been describing to you all center around you and your supposed happiness. Remember, Philippians is about joy. If you want to know what real joy is, you have to get busy dying, dying to yourself, dying to your way, dying to your wants, dying to sin. Jesus died for sin once and for all, for our salvation. As we grow in Christ, we must die to the daily sin that still tempts us and tries to fool us into thinking we do it for joy. Paul repeatedly announces that Christ died for us and our sin. Look:

> For while we were still weak, at the right time Christ died for the ungodly.
> -Romans 5:6

> ...but God shows his love for us in that while we were still sinners, Christ died for us.　　　　　-Romans 5:8

> Now if we have died with Christ, we believe that we will also live with him.
> -Romans 6:8

> For the death he died he died to sin, once for all, but the life he lives he lives to God.　　　　-Romans 6:10

> For to this end Christ died and lived again, that he might be Lord both of the dead and of the living.　　-Romans 14:9

Paul was in jail. It wasn't a five-star hotel with resort accommodations or a country club type "Club Fed." The conditions were horrible, deplorable. I'm sure there were
24

rats and infestation of all kinds. Disease, sickness, and the stench of death lingered in the air. How did he cope? Paul had died to himself. He had died to sin. He died to his own way, and he was living God's way. If he had demanded his way, he wouldn't have been living God's way. The only way to really live and find joy is to die to sin. Sin disguises itself to you and me. It has the appearance of joy, but it's a deadly lie and only an apparition of the truth. The answer is dying unto God. Don't you see Paul's attitude: "It really doesn't matter to me what happens. If I get out of this jail cell, I win. If I die I win!"

True living is when you are no longer concerned with your circumstances and find your joy in wanting to please God with your obedient living. Turning from sin is as important as turning to Christ.

Consider this analogy. It's the life so many Christians have settled for:

A young couple gets married, and friends get together and give them a luxurious all-expense paid honeymoon to Bermuda! It's in the middle of the summertime, the pristine blue water is crystal-clear and sparkles off of the sandy surf. It's beautiful there (they tell me). The couple has been given one of those penthouse, presidential suites with a panoramic view, where you can literally wake up in the morning watching the sun come up and go to bed watching it go down while you sip Mimosas. The wait staff brings you breakfast in bed. You can sunbathe and eat shrimp cocktail all day long. The comforts of this place are incredible! Massages and mani-pedis are free every day.

But the friends who purchased the package bought the flight to Bermuda for that dream honeymoon with a stopover in Newark.

The only hotel available was a slum, flea and bedbug infested room. In order to spend 12 days in paradise, a five-star hotel, they first must have to spend the night in roach motel.

They don't even give stars to rate this place. It's just nasty. It's gross. And it's the only way to get there— the only flight and only hotel that comes along with this deal. Most people can't wait to get out of there or don't even close their eyes if they even lay in the bed. The next morning, the bride looks at her groom and says, "Honey, why don't we just stay here?"

What?! Are you joking? That's an insult, that's grounds for divorce! Before you start thinking the new bride has lost her mind, it's exactly what we do to God and His promise for joy and opulent living when we refuse to die to sin. We are guilty of precisely the same thing when we settle for the nastiness of sin and for less than what God has for us, instead of trusting Him and following Him all the way.

Jonathan Edwards, that great Puritan preacher and first president of Princeton, considered by so many the greatest academic mind America ever produced said,

> That's the way we are. We are like travelers that set out for a glorious destination and they stop at a run-down inn on the way, and you have to pull them away out of that inn to get them to go to their final destination.

That's the way we are when we don't know Christ. We are lost. We are living busy lives that don't count, and pretty soon we will be dead.

3. Get Busy with Jesus - Hurry to Joy

God nailed our sins to the Cross along with His Son, and His Son died. Unless you kill your sins— allow Jesus to take them from you and kill them— you will never truly live. You will never experience Godly joy.

How? How do I get to that level of joy that God wants so much for me? **Get busy living for Jesus by...**

...daily putting to death the sin in your life...

...then you will be on your way to true joy in Christ. Every day you need to preach to yourself that Jesus died for your sins. For emphasis, let me put it in bold: **EVERY. DAY.**

Remember what I said about stopping the hurry in your life? That was the hurry in living for yourself, or trying to rush God. It's quite the opposite when we consider the state of joy. Don't waste your time getting to joy! Hurry! Hurry to the Cross of Christ, lay down your life, allow Him to kill off your sinful past and narcissistic self. Hurry to repent and turn to Him in right living. Hurry up and do it today!

In Paul's greeting to the church at Philippi he was torn over coming or going. He wanted to come to the church and enjoy the fellowship of believers and for them to hang out in wonderful fellowship with each other while building them up. But at the same time, he realized that joy with the Father in heaven awaits. What to do? What would you do? It's a great thing to get to a point when you are contemplating whether to stay here with the body of Christ or go home to God, and both are joy. Peace and joy to you as you seek Him.

➡

Chapter 2 – JOY123 Study Guide:

J1 How have you been slow to obey **JESUS** and live a right life? How can you get in a hurry to serve Him without living a hurried and frenzied life for Him? Can you do this for the rest of the year? Write down the areas in your life where you are going too fast, so that they are before you, and you can pray to God to slow you down to experience real joy:

_____

_____

_____

_____

_____

_____

_____

_____

_____

_____

_____

_____

_____

_____

02 One of the best ways to treat **OTHERS** is to give them undivided time and attention. Listen to **OTHERS** and encourage them in the name of Jesus.

Find someone this week that you would otherwise overlook or hurry through a conversation with, and spend time with them.

- Look them in the eyes when you listen
- Block out your selfishness
- Resist trying to talk over them
- Praying with them makes you a true friend
- Write them a letter of encouragement or prayer

Y3 YOU don't get to the point of slowing down without practice. Practice being patient. Practice being obedient. Practice listening to God as you read His holy Word. **YOU** will see joy begin to build in your life.

Write out the answer to this question: If you had one hour a day to spend with God, where you were not interrupted, and you know you wouldn't be penalized for not doing something else, and where you know that hour would pay off, how would you spend it? If you already do this, complete the exercise anyway. You may see ways you can improve it!

_____
_____
_____
_____
_____
_____
_____
_____
_____
_____
_____
_____
_____
_____
_____

Chapter 3

Massive

*And being found in human form, <u>he
humbled himself</u> by becoming obedient to
the point of death, even death on a cross.*
-Philippians 2:8

*...[N]eighborly love is that we must not
merely will our neighbors good, but
actually work to bring it about.*
-Thomas Aquinas

Neighborly love is something you can't just talk about.
You have to do it. If you say you are a good neighbor, then
you have committed yourself to being a good friend instead
of just being there lingering. I'm not talking about the "like a
good neighbor..." insurance company, but a true neighbor.

The church needs to return to the basics and really
love people by seeking to do acts of kindness and love.
Loving your neighbor is practical living and not a
beforehand feeling. The church finds joy in serving her
neighbors. That kind of service means preaching and
presenting Jesus at every turn. A church will explode in joy
and growth when they strive to attract neighbors to Christ
rather than to themselves.

You've missed the point if you think that church is nothing but this religious gig going on in our town or city where we just host our own little get togethers trying to outdo the local entertainment. If you think we are to put all these hours into preparing, and working, so that we can check off our Christian duty each week, then you have grossly misinterpreted the vision. Yes, you've surely misread us if you think we are into a bigger, better style of worship, more church stuff, larger crowds, and overcrowded parking areas. The real church is about the highest calling ever known to man. In the history of recorded time, there hasn't been a more important agenda. It's God's agenda, it's His plan. We go to where He leads. We are here to magnify Jesus and lift Him up in everything we do. That, my friend, is finding real joy in church work.

In a little more detail: Through Jesus Christ, His only Son, because of His sacrificial death on a tree two thousand years ago, subsequently rising from the dead, with a Resurrected body, and from His own lips, "Go and share and make disciples..." we— *us*— are commissioned. And if you are a Christ-follower, you are sworn in, equipped, have been given marching orders. And so we are in the middle of going. The church world is inundated with plans, blueprints, and ideas on how to sprout a church. A quick Google search will put you in touch with hundreds of outfits ready to sell you their philosophy on church growth. It has become a multi-million-dollar business. I can't buy into it anymore.

From this fantastic section of Scripture in Philippians chapter 2, verse 8, we see some down-home teaching from the Apostle Paul. Motivation and direction come from Holy Scripture. This isn't some lofty sermon that you will have to interpret. No, this is country cooking at its finest from the New Testament book of Philippians.

The New Testament has twenty-seven books. The first four are the Gospels. They recount the story of Jesus and His life, His teaching of life and what life is all about, and surely what the kingdom is all about. Acts is the book of action, complete with miraculous signs. It is also the beginning of the church and shows what God did through those first disciples. Most of the rest of the New Testament is doctrine for the church: how we are to act, live, proceed, worship, obey, give, serve, and love. There are specifics for those things in the body, the church, and living in this community, this lost world.

Saint Thomas Aquinas lays the foundation for us: It's not enough, he says, to hope for a good neighborhood, but instead it is your duty, my duty, our duty and commission by Jesus, to bring it about. This world is a dark place. What if— just what if— some church decided they were going to reach and teach Jesus to the fullest in just the community they lived in? How will that change your neighborhood?

The world says believe in yourself, put yourself first, don't trust anyone, stash your money away, and retire early. Contemporary social structures define greatness with largeness. Never before has the phrase, "the more the merrier" been more apt in describing modern society than it is today. But here the Apostle Paul (remember, writing from prison) says,

> *So if there is any encouragement in Christ, any comfort from love, any participation in the Spirit, any affection and sympathy, complete my joy by being of the same mind, having the same love, being in full accord and of one mind. Do nothing from selfish ambition or conceit, but in humility count others more significant than yourselves. Let each of you look not only to his own interests, but also to the interests of others. Have this mind among yourselves, which is yours in Christ Jesus, who, though he was in the form of God, did*

not count equality with God a thing to be grasped, but emptied himself, by taking the form of a servant, being born in the likeness of men. And being found in human form, he humbled himself by becoming obedient to the point of death, even death on a cross.

-Philippians 2:1-8

Two Massive Statements on Humility:

1. Greatness comes by serving others

Make no mistake, the backdrop of all of Paul's letters have to do with the greatness of our Lord. You can see it throughout chapter 2 of Philippians. If it is not built in us to be great in Christ, then advertisements and social media will take over and demand that we do stuff to be great like the world. Those things usually mean carving your own way— it's just the opposite of Scripture. Big and extravagant is good sometimes, but it is our God that is immense, not our productions of Him. God isn't impressed with all of those things if you are not serving others.

In Acts 17, Paul meets the smart people. He encounters the Greek philosophers in Athens. These guys sat around every day making wise comments... and they got paid for it! Paul walked around for a while observing the different statues of gods in the town. Then, he rubbed his eyes, scratched his head, and mused over one plaque whose inscription read, "To the unknown god." It was the Greek way of saying, "If we have neglected a god, wrongly omitted one out there, then we don't want to leave them out, so we apologize and have set up a catch-all altar to him or her."

Instead of making a mockery of it by laughing in their faces, Paul used it to preach a powerful sermon. He describes the greatness of God in a way the world doesn't consider in their resistance of Him. Paul boldly announced,

> *The God who made the world and everything in it, being Lord of heaven and earth, does not live in temples made by man, nor is he served by human hands, as though he needed anything, since he himself gives to all mankind life and breath and everything.*

Paul is saying that just because you can't imagine Him or see Him doesn't mean He doesn't live, and He lives greatly.

Many modern churches want to declare victory, so every week they will post the numbers of attendance and those who were baptized or made a profession of faith. I suppose that's great, but many like to tout their own greatness. If you are not serving, then you are not really a great church. When a church brags on the stuff they do on a massive scale, then you should look for the little things. Greatness in any organization means there is someone who is paying attention to the details, doing things behind the scenes where they seldom receive credit. But true believers don't want credit anyway.

You can't talk about being a true neighbor without talking about the Good Samaritan. Over the years I've referenced it so much that I should be weary of it, but it's pure sweetness and I never tire of it.

Appreciate that as Jesus tells the story there is an audience. And if the speaker doesn't know his audience, he can't make a great point. This particular audience is the religious crowd, the church folks. So, you assume that they know how to act, right? Yes, and Jesus knew that they knew how they were to act.

Let's quickly go back into the Old Testament and you see exactly how you are to treat your neighbor...

...Don't just stand by when your neighbor's life is in danger. I am God.

Don't secretly hate your neighbor. If you have something against him, get it out into the open; otherwise you are an accomplice in his guilt. Don't seek revenge or carry a grudge against any of your people. Love your neighbor as yourself. I am God. —Leviticus 19:16-18

Now, to Jesus' story of the Good Samaritan: A man traveling the Jericho road is robbed and thrown in the ditch for dead. First a religious man, a preacher, comes by, looks ahead and sees the man lying in the ditch and avoids him by crossing to the other side. Next, Jesus says, one of the man's brothers, a man of the same race, sees him and also avoids him. Finally a Samaritan, the sworn enemy of the Jews, goes down into the ditch, helps the man, gets him a place to stay and medical help while he convalesces, even paying all his bills. Jesus asks, "Which one is the neighbor?" You see, they knew! Jesus knew they knew... and they knew He knew what they knew. But talking about it and doing it are two different things. The stranger was the true neighbor because he did right. He did the neighborly things.

The church in America today is not going to be great just because we do great stuff on a great scale with great money in front of great crowds. No, we are going to be great by serving our community with the Gospel message. Strangers at first, maybe, but we will all become family. If you want to be great in the eyes of your Father in heaven... serve!

➲

2. Oneness cannot be achieved without humility

Look at these statements from Philippians 2:

- ➲ Do nothing from selfish ambition or conceit
- ➲ Count others more significant than yourselves
- ➲ Have this mind among yourselves, which is yours in Christ Jesus, who, though he was in the form of God, did not count equality with God a thing to be grasped
- ➲ He emptied himself, by taking the form of a servant
- ➲ He humbled himself by becoming obedient to the point of death, even death on a cross

If I could advise younger pastors and church staff I would say, "Please, modern day church, quit trying to become the superstar church. We don't need Jesus Christ Superstar. We don't need that thinking. We already have the Super One in Christ Jesus." We need to believe and understand that when our pride takes the stage, then Jesus walks off. When we turn the lights onto ourselves, we have dimmed the true light in our lives. He is the One we are to magnify. It's what Paul is trying to communicate as he conveys to the church the importance of being humble. Put others ahead of yourself. Love them. When we love others, we are loving Him. Let's examine the statements from this passage in chapter 2:

➲ **Nothing from Selfish Ambition** – We are all at least a little selfish. Many of us have a lot of ambition. Some of us are conceited. All that is a given. But when it comes to the church, you have to pull that antecedent back into the picture so that none of us will get the big head when it comes to His family. Go back to Chapter One and see who the letter is addressed to. It's addressed to us, the church. Just because you give more money, just because you get there early before everyone else, just because you parked in the best space, just because you lead on the stage every Sunday, it doesn't mean you should seek to be proud. God's plan for us is to be one, and you can't be one when you are in it for yourself.

➲ **Count others more significant** – If we are going to be one together— celebrate together, worship together, experience pain together, pray together, laugh together— then we are going to have to start putting the needs of others before ourselves. It's the Christian way, the only way. "Pastor, how?"

Jesus did it. This is that famous passage of Scripture where we are told that Jesus did it. He left glory, He left His seat in the heavenlies, He left paradise, He left the Father's right hand, and He left! Think of the fact that He was in a place where He was served all day long, yet He left in order to serve. You can't say it any better than the Lord Jesus,

> *Do you want to stand out? Then step down. Be a servant. If you puff yourself up, you'll get the wind knocked out of you. But if you're content to simply be yourself, your life will count for plenty.*
> *-Matthew 23:11-12 (The Message)*

➲ **Have this mind** – What mind? Christ's mind. I don't think whose mind it means registers with us when we read it. Paul is talking about the mind of Christ. You and I are to have the mind of Christ. I was watching a preacher on Facebook the other day, a young guy, and he says, "God told me...." And it was some nebulous, vague thing to make himself sound important. I believe God talks to us. Through His Word. Don't think there is a certain level or depth in Christianity where once you serve long enough, or when you release enough of your so-called faith upwards to the heavens, that you are going to begin to hear spiritual voices that come to you and to no one else. If you are going to align yourself in importance with an Old Testament prophet in speaking to God, then you better be correct one hundred percent of the time! How subjective is it to believe God speaks these outside words predicting social, global, or political happenings? What is the mind of Christ? We know it by knowing God's Word. The book of Hebrews opens like this:

> *Going through a long line of prophets, God has been addressing our ancestors in different ways for centuries. Recently he spoke to us directly through his Son. By his Son, God created the world in the beginning, and it will all belong to the Son at the end. This Son perfectly mirrors God, and is stamped with God's nature. He holds everything together by what he says— powerful words!*
> *-Hebrews 1:1-3 (The Message)*

➲ **Emptied Himself** – My grandfather used to say, "You're full of yourself." That definitely describes our world and the selfishness of people. The die-hard Beatles fan knows it's been over fifty years since the band broke up, and I'm convinced that the catalyst of their breakup was spiritual. No, I don't think they were ever close to Christianity, apart from growing up Catholic. But Paul encouraged the group to go to India in search of a guru to take them to some other, quasi-spiritual, level, and George selfishly clung to it. He became a Krishna follower and from that point on his songs reflected that cultish sound. You see, when our search for spirituality starts from a selfish perspective— to gain more information, so as to be more full of ourselves— we will not know the true Savior. The true Savior, Jesus, modeled it for us by emptying Himself. In other words, He served. Those disciples in the Gospel story of Jesus bowing in front of them with a pail of water just couldn't get over the fact that He was washing their feet! But leadership is couched by humility and servanthood. True leadership is found in the sum of humility and servanthood.

➲ **He humbled himself by becoming obedient** – How was Jesus obedient? Did He say "Yes, sir" and "No, sir" to God? Was He obedient by eating the right stuff? By not cussing? By being sweet and kind and nice and loving and pure and smiling all of the time? That's usually what we think about when we consider obedience. Was He obedient by always doing the right thing? In a simplistic way, all those things are true. But that is not what Paul was going after...not at all. How are we obedient? When Paul is talking to us, the church, and when he is talking about this Scripture, he is dealing with you and me. He is telling us that Jesus obeyed God all the way, in everything, even when the Father told Him to die for us on the Roman Cross! Humbling ourselves to obedience is our work and our goal in life.

Where is the joy in this passage of Scripture? Paul prefaces it all by saying, "complete my joy." I imagine this analogous scenario: Paul is eating dinner in a southern restaurant and is drinking iced tea. Sweet tea, mind you.

And the server keeps returning and returning and topping off his glass. It never gets empty. In the same way, Paul is saying, "Fill up my joy and keep filling it up by doing these things, and my joy will be completely complete."

Joy is not just a matter of you being good, and doing the right thing. It is that God has called you and me to die to sin. There is no negotiation in this. If you are seeking joy in your life, dealing with sin isn't just chapter one and then we move on. Not at all. For years and years preachers have tried to soften the blow. The church has tried to make God more palatable to our American tastes, and more attractive to those outside of Christ. But I always end up here at the end of a message: There is a direct correlation between your dealing with sin, and the joy in your life. Your glass of joy will always be half empty if you continue to avoid it. Make your joy complete by humbling yourself before Him.

Chapter 3 – **JOY123** Study Guide:

J1 Examine and study how **JESUS** was humble in everything He did. Look at these particular passages from the Gospels, then pick one and write down what you learn from Jesus:

- ➲ Matthew 18:4
- ➲ Luke 14:11
- ➲ Matthew 21:5
- ➲ Matthew 20:25-28

_____
_____
_____
_____

_____

_____

_____

_____

_____

_____

02 Sometimes we try to impress others with our travels, riches, or social status. We engage in humble-brag about our possessions. I dare you to start humbling yourself before **OTHERS** by encouraging others instead of trying to "one-up" them.

Here's an exercise: pray and ask God why you have the possessions you enjoy while others have less. Write down 5-10 of those *things* you have and evaluate them on a scale of 1 to 10 (10 being that which you cannot part with):

_____

_____

_____

_____

_____

_____

_____

_____

Y3 YOU and your heart will mislead **YOU**. Seek to have the mind of Christ by praying and asking God for direction in every decision in your life. In what one area today do you need His direction and wisdom?

_____

_____

_____

_____

Chapter 4

Every

Therefore God has highly exalted him and bestowed on him the name that is above every name, so that at the name of Jesus every knee should bow, in heaven and on earth and under the earth, and every tongue confess that Jesus Christ is Lord, to the glory of God the Father.

-Philippians 2:9-11

Here's your sign. You see and experience it every day traveling down life's highway, walking out of a local business, or signing out of your social media page:

Usually long before a basketball game has ended, I am headed for the exit. I don't like to stick around for all of the postgame festivities. I try to time it just right, judging the score and seeing if the victory has been secured, so I can get out of the arena and dodge the traffic. My wife and I have a code for when we want to exit a party or gathering. It's a secret code— I can't tell you what it is. We covertly flash it to one another, and make our way to the exit, or the car.

Brexit is Great Britain's attempt to leave the European Union. Britain joined the EU, an economic and political union of twenty-eight European countries, in 1973. Then a few years ago, they voted to get out, to exit, to leave.

On the heels of Brexit came *Megxit.* The new princess, Meghan Markle, married Prince Harry several years ago and...well, they have decided to exit. They want to walk away from the royal atmosphere and live in North America. It's become a huge deal. Think about this: you marry into royalty and all you have to do is get up every day and smile for the queen. You live absolutely in the lap of luxury. You live in castles, you travel on private jets, you ride around in a Rolls-Royce, all of your meals are prepared for you, all of your laundry is washed, folded, and fluffed. You stay at the best hotels and resorts while eating caviar and drinking champagne. You get all the best medical care in the world— they even come to your castle for the treatment. You get to do anything you want to do as long as you smile for the queen, and then no bills, no work, no struggles. But Harry and Meghan have decided to exit— to leave.

When God deals with us in our lives, He is talking about entering our lives, which stands counter to our contemplation about exiting this world. Which do you think about more— entering or exiting? Many folks weigh their options for getting out of the pressures of this life. Suicide statistics are off the charts as a way to escape or exit. However, the Christ-follower knows the answer is found in entering God's Kingdom, and having the Holy Spirit indwell you and me. Have you ever casually walked up to a door at a restaurant or a store and pulled the handle to go in, only to discover it's the exit and the door won't open? Yeah, you have. And in embarrassment, hoping no one was looking, you quickly turned toward the other door.

44

It seems so many of us are looking to exit life's experiences and pressures for something meaningful. We want to exit the work force with retirement, understandable when you reach your 60's. There are those who want to exit relationships, commitments, contracts, their life situations. Yet we do not plan for the exit from this planet, at the end of our days, when we draw our final breath. Some of us are on this freeway of life, speeding down the highway, singing *I Can't Drive 55* and never understanding that, one day, we are going to have to exit.

In this joy-seeking book of Philippians, Paul was writing to the church he started in Europe. Scholars and theologians debate whether the words in Philippians 2:9-11 were a song that the early Christians sang, or whether they were original words of Paul. There's something about these three verses that are different from the rest of the letter.

Take a look at this list that summarizes the whole story— all 66 books of the Bible— the Gospel— in five seconds or less:

- Creation
- The Fall
- Condescension
- Crucifixion
- Resurrection
- Redemption

You may believe that is where the story ends, but if you do you would be grossly deluded and deprived of crucial information pertaining to your joyful state as a Christ-follower. Look at these terms as they lead us to grasp the three terrific verses in Paul's letter:

- Ascension
- Coronation/Exaltation
- Consummation

➲ Restoration

We tend to think that after the Resurrection, there is nothing else. After Jesus rose from the dead, and we placed our faith and trust in Him, forsaking our sin, and living for Him, that...that's it. But zoom in on God the King and the King maker, and focus on the terms *ascension* and *coronation* (*exaltation*) that we find here. The crowning of the King is massive to our understanding of Paul's message of joy. His royal highness has been overlooked or taken for granted. The book of Hebrews paints the royal picture:

> *He is the radiance of the glory of God and the exact imprint of his nature, and he upholds the universe by the word of his power. After making purification for sins, he sat down at the right hand of the Majesty on high.* -Hebrews 1:3

The Hebrew writer says the coronation includes the seating of the Son. Before Jesus was crowned with glory, in glory by the Father (and being born King), He was crowned with thorns by you and me.

They say that Prince Harry and Meghan gave up their royal crowns for Hollywood living... bless their hearts. Crowns are important to some people. In royal succession, in pageants, and in the beauty queen world, the crown is a big deal. It's enormous to God also, but we are talking about a very different sort of crown. It's huge to your life and mine because God is talking about who you and I follow and bow down to. Can you remember that line from the great hymn, "Holy, Holy, Holy" that says,

> *"Holy, holy, holy! All the saints adore thee, casting down their golden crowns around the glassy sea..."*

A few chapters on in Hebrews, we're told Jesus was crowned with glory because of His suffering. Philippians 2 allows us to peek in on more of that coronation ceremony taking place in the heavenlies. Paul is encouraging us to bear our burdens in humility. You and me.

Struggling in this world could be the number one most confusing thing to believers about following Jesus. For those who endure, for those who take up their cross, for those who remain steadfast, and for those who recognize that they are going through it— keep going! You are going to go through difficult times, so recognize it and keep trusting, realizing your faith builds the character of Christ in you and that the payoff is oh so good. Scripture identifies something called the "crown of life" or the "crown of glory." I can't say specifically what that crown is, nor can I describe it, but I have never heard of anything associated with the crown, or any crown, that was not fantastic. Look at these uplifting verses:

> *Blessed is the man who remains steadfast under trial, for when he has stood the test he **will receive the crown of life**, which God has promised to those who love him.* *−James 1:12*

> *And when the chief Shepherd appears, you will receive the* ***unfading crown of glory.*** *−1 Peter 5:4*

> *Do not fear what you are about to suffer. Behold, the devil is about to throw some of you into prison, that you may be tested, and for ten days you will have tribulation. Be faithful unto death, and **I will give you the crown of life**. −Revelation 2:10*

Yes, we who are in Christ are going to get a crown. A crown always means a position of honor. But does that really matter when you are in the presence of the Lord Jesus? The old hymn writer wrote these words, and even though the words are not Scriptural, I believe they are a glimpse into heaven itself:

> *"Holy, holy, holy! All the saints adore thee,*
> *casting down their golden crowns around*
> *the glassy sea;*
> *Cherubim and seraphim falling down*
> *before thee, who wert, and art, and*
> *evermore shalt be."*

The picture we get from this song is that when you see Jesus, in His glory, your pure gold crown is immaterial to you. A few million dollars would be chump change to trade for a foretaste of glory divine. Your status as being elevated to heaven will pale in comparison to being in the presence of the Almighty. All of the royal benefits don't add up to much when you are in the company of the Creator. I believe all the joy we have in this life is just a taste of what will come when we see Him face to face.

If you are having doubts about your relationship with God, and if you are confused about salvation from God, then this next part is just for you. It's where most of twenty-first century America has missed God, and where the church continues to miss Him.

My statement on the Royal Highness: Jesus is King. He is King Jesus. It's advantageous for us to speak of Him as our Savior. He is. It's cool to talk about Him as our friend. He is. What a friend we have in Jesus. It's nice to think of Him as right here with us through it all. Yes, God has sent the Holy Spirit to walk with us. But, somehow, we have missed the majesty part. Get this: He is— majestic!

I like cool church, sometimes, where our translations of the Bible have made the language understandable, where we can wear jeans with holes in them to church while drinking coffee and looking hip while we watch the guitarist wail like Angus Young of AC/DC. But that doesn't mean that we can be flippant with God.

As a tot, I learned early on not to run in the church building, especially not in the sanctuary, narthex, and foyer (I still don't know what a narthex is!). I know there's that thing of older people not liking the wild shenanigans of children, but it was more than that. My grandparents equated being in a church with being in a holy place, and it is to a big degree. Maybe that is the problem. We've let the children run in the narthex. We have de-sanctified God. We have un-holied and corrupted our approach and presence before God. Taking the holy and making it sacrilegious leads to terrible consequences. It may look harmless, and may help us meet our numbers goals, but what is it doing to the body of Christ? When we no longer shake before the holy God we will do what we want to do, when we want to do it. Here's an exercise for you: using a word finder in a Bible app, read the passages where the word *tremble* appears. When we no longer fear the Lord, we take matters into our own hands and make our presence before Him stink to the highest cloud. The way some of us act and behave in front of God, I am shocked He doesn't do away with more of us every day!

It scares me these days the way some churches conduct the Lord's Supper. There are far too many that play around with it. It's supposed to be a holy time when we confess and get real by remembering the agony, the shame, the embarrassment, and pain that He suffered on the Cross. But not these days. We should tremble as we take the cup representing His blood shed for us. But instead we act as if it's just another ho-hum custom. We think if we do it then we please Him when, if we don't approach it with reverence, just the opposite is true. It should be that place where we pause and ask ourselves, "Am I right with God?" And if we are not, then we use it as a sermon to our souls to get right. The Bible is clear,

> Whoever, therefore, eats the bread or drinks the cup of the Lord in an unworthy manner will be guilty concerning the body and blood of the Lord. Let a person examine himself, then, and so eat of the bread and drink of the cup. For anyone who eats and drinks without discerning the body eats and drinks judgment on himself. That is why many of you are weak and ill, and some have died.   -1 Corinthians 11:27-30

Do you know anyone who died unexpectedly even though they went to church all their lives? You have to wonder.

This little hymn, in these three verses in Philippians 2, is important to our knowledge of eternal joy. Notice the wording, notice the word *every*.

Every Name

> Therefore God has highly exalted him and bestowed on him the name that is above **every** name...

What name? Jesus? No. *Lord*. It's a coronation name. It's an exaltation name. It means master, it means owner. Jesus doesn't tell those stories about owners and servants in the Gospels for the fun of it or for you to feel some religious goosebumps. He is describing the Kingdom of God, and when you have a Kingdom, you have a King! He is Lord of all. It means that He is super-exalted. He has received the place of honor and majesty and is seated at the right hand of the Father.

50

Recall the incident when the mother of James and John comes to Jesus and says, "Hey, I want you to let my boys sit on your right and left...I want them to flank you, I want them to be the most important in the Kingdom." Jesus says, "You don't have a clue what you are asking. And if you did, it's not my decision, it's the Father's!" Read the account in Matthew 20 and you will see Jesus has just announced to His disciples that He is going to the Cross. And, in this most inopportune time in human history, the mother of the boys of Zebedee blurts out her little inconsequential greedy request. Instead of it being a time for the disciples to bow at His Lordship, it turned into a little ruckus over who is the greatest. Do you see it? James and John were going to bow before King Jesus, but they wanted to know who was going to bow down to them!

Exaltation is the opposite of humiliation. He who stood condemned has exchanged it for the seat of righteousness. He who was poor is now rich. He who was rejected has been accepted. He who learned obedience now administrates it. His name is above every name. Your joy will flee off into the night when you seek to elevate yourself above others in this world. What joy there is in knowing there is no other name above His! Our joy comes from knowing that as far as the planets stretch, and as far as galaxies extend, He is in charge and there is no one else!

Every Knee

...so that at the name of Jesus every knee should bow, in heaven and on earth and under the earth....

Where do some come off thinking they are co-owners with God? We don't own this church. We haven't bought into a pyramid scheme where we will achieve some type of proud status with big monetary rewards to follow. At His return, all created beings will worship Him. It may take until then for some of us to get it but, Lord, I hope not. The angels and those of us who are redeemed in Christ, those who have been changed by Him and acknowledge His glory, will bow before Him. And those... those who despise Him, who hate Him, who have resisted Him— in other words, the damned— will do so ruefully and remorsefully. It will not be done penitently, that is, apologetically realizing that He is God and finally bowing. No, they will still resist.

> *One day Jesus is going to return and every knee will bow, and those that don't He will break their knee with the rod.*
>
> *-RC Sproul*

You may think this is disturbing, and question it's meaning. You might say, "I thought Jesus was all lovey-dovey, sweet and forgiving and we could be cool and drink our Budweiser and smoke our dope and He still loves us, and that He just wants this relationship with us...and all that stuff." Think again. If I know nothing else about joy and His Kingdom, I know this: God is happy. He is joyful and He enjoys His creation. Scripture paints a very vivid picture of our just, yet merciful, God. He is the King— King Jesus. One day He is coming, and He won't come riding side-saddle on a multi-colored unicorn. No, here's how He is coming, as John the Revelator explains,

> *Then I saw heaven opened, and behold, a white horse! The one sitting on it is called Faithful and True, and in righteousness he judges and makes war. His eyes are like a flame of fire, and on his head are many diadems, and he has a name written that no one knows but himself. He is clothed in a robe dipped in blood, and the name by which he is called*

is The Word of God. And the armies of heaven, arrayed in fine linen, white and pure, were following him on white horses. From his mouth comes a sharp sword with which to strike down the nations, and he will rule them with a rod of iron. He will tread the winepress of the fury of the wrath of God the Almighty."

-Revelation 19:11-15

Every single knee will bow...every single one.

Every Tongue

"...and every tongue confess that Jesus Christ is Lord, to the glory of God the Father."

Every tongue. Every single tongue.

There was a king one time who loved his bride, he loved his wife so much. He dressed her in beautiful gowns of white reflecting her purity and simplicity. He had to go away and let's just say he called you, a servant, to take care of her. He wasn't flippant about how to care for his beloved. He left explicit, detailed instructions on how to serve her and even outlined what not to do. Every jot and tittle he outlined unambiguously. Seems simple enough, doesn't it?

However, he was gone longer than you, the servant, and others expected. A very long time. And the people grew tired of the king because he hadn't kept up with the times and become cool like them. And they became tired of the bride because she isn't cool, either. She hasn't adapted to the culture and changed to be modern and fashionable. So, many of the subjects take a hike. They leave. But you, the servant, are quite clever. You now decide that the king needs help with his image. He needs a makeover. And, you decide to redecorate, revamp, redesign, and remodel his bride's image. You take off her fine white linens, off with the veil, take away the chiffon and silk. You take down her hair, you paint her face, you sparkle her with adornments. Out with the old-fashioned, and in with the contemporary.

But in reality, you've dressed her like a whore. You have cheapened her, giving her a bargain-basement-price feel. You parade her around in front of the carnal, worldly-thinking men of the kingdom, hoping they will think she is cool now and that this will convince them to recommence their loyalty to the king. You market her the same way you would market some new product to be sold on television or the Internet. The musicians playing around her pulse in with their new sound and new beat. It's crude, is it not?

But it's exactly what a multitude of evangelical pastors and churches are doing today. What will happen to that servant when the king returns? The king will kill him. What will the King do when He comes back for you? Well, if we decide we need to modernize, entertain, add to His instructions, and draw people in by raising the hem of the church's skirt, then know this: it will be better for the hostile atheist than it will be for us.

If you don't glean but one thing from this chapter, please latch on to this: He is King Jesus.

> *The Lord sits enthroned over the flood;*
> *the Lord sits enthroned as king forever.*
> *May the Lord give strength to his people!*
> *May the Lord bless his people with*
> *peace!* —Psalm 29:10-11

You will understand the joy Jesus wants you to have when you understand that He is our Royal Highness. He is on His throne. No one comes against Him or is able. Jesus is Lord. When we live in this, we live in His presence. He gives peace to us, to His people. That is joy, a joy unspeakable.

Chapter 4 – **JOY123** Study Guide:

01 For joy, for fun, list here as many attributes or adjectives for **JESUS** and His royalty as you can, use the Bible if you want. Here's a hint: Go to the Psalms and scour the pages and you will find what you are looking for. Keep the list in your Bible, referring to them as often as possible to describe His Royal Highness. If you are putting Jesus first, you'd better know who He is!

_____

_____

_____

_____

_____

_____

_____

_____

_____

_____

_____

_____

_____

_____

02 Tell **OTHERS** about your loyalty to royalty, your devotion to Jesus. Find out how your friends view King Jesus and be encouraging to them to seek God. Write down what they say. It will help you understand where people come from and how to effectively share the Gospel with others:

_____

_____

_____

_____
_____
_____
_____
_____
_____
_____

Y3 YOU will bow before Him when He returns or you will go to see Him. Get in some practice sessions by getting on your knees and thanking Him for all He has done for you. List the ways He has blessed **YOU** recently. I promise it will bring you joy:

_____
_____
_____
_____
_____
_____
_____
_____
_____
_____
_____
_____
_____
_____
_____
_____

Chapter 5

Spiritual Muscle

Therefore, my beloved, as you have always obeyed, so now, not only as in my presence but much more in my absence, work out your own salvation with fear and trembling, for it is God who works in you, both to will and to work for his good pleasure.   *-Philippians 2:12-13*

Do you have a workout routine? Exercise, jog, lift weights, Jazzercise, yoga, Pilates, FightCamp, or P90x? For some time now, our pop culture has been subjected to pictures of incredible physiques, with six-pack abs, chiseled pecs, and cut calf muscles minus the fat, and their advertisement is that if you buy their product, then you can have that same certain look. If you work out and diet then you, too, can have that amazing body. Or, if you purchase their routine, their plan, their workout, for the low, low price of $99.99— in 48 installments— then you can be incredible too.

Have you noticed that gym memberships are on the decline? It's true. People are discovering that they can get in shape at home cheaper. So, to combat that, gyms have begun letting you join month-to-month. Do you remember the days when you had to sign a 30-year contract to join a gym? I was even sued once for breaking a gym contract because I moved out of that town. It was crazy!

The gym fad all started with an Italian guy, Angelo Siciliano. You may know him as Charles Atlas. Here's how the story goes: Angelo was a 97-pound weakling and one day, on the beach, some bigger kid kicked sand in his face embarrassing him in front of the girls. So he decided to start working out with weights. In 1922, they said he had the most defined body in the world. That was only the beginning. Arnold Schwarzenegger took it to another level in the 1970's by becoming Mr. Olympia seven times with Joe Weider training him. And today, after working out with Jack LaLanne, Jane Fonda, Denise Austin, Richard Simmons, and Tony Little... today's stars, and they are many... we have this term: *workout*.

Do you work out? I work out frequently. I notice I am slowing down and my body doesn't want to do it anymore—not like it did when I was in my thirties and forties. Now it has become mind over matter. Now there is a certain message (sermon) I have to preach to myself. It goes like this:

Hey Greg, you are getting old. Yeah, your hair is getting grey...and falling out too! You have this spare tire that means that you have to buy a 36 waist-size. I know for the last ten years you have been a 36, but you buy 34s and squeeze into them. You used to be able to eat a gallon of ice cream every night and it didn't show. Now, you have to get used to celery and carrots.

Hey Greg, the scales don't lie! You are that fat. You are slowing down. Your muscles are shrinking. You are losing your memory. Your vision is dimming. Your teeth will fall out if you make it to 100. So get up and quit complaining.

Get up and run. Lace up the shoes, put down the Snickers, quit buying 2-for-1 gallon ice creams, stop going to the buffets, and enjoy the broccoli, cauliflower, and brussels sprouts... if you want to feel good.

I have to tell myself that every day. Or something like it. And let me tell you how I respond to myself sometimes, "Take a hike Greg! This cheeseburger and fries tastes too good! Besides, these new elastic waist stretch pants work just fine." But, on some occasions, I heed my own advice and work out. I think it's important.   The Apostle Paul tells Timothy, *"Working out is good, but not as good as growing in godliness."* I want you to know about growing in godliness. Because if you are not spiritually working out, then you are developing a lot of spiritual flab, and that flab is weighing you down from knowing God. And in the same way being a couch potato puts on the pounds, when you avoid and devoid your life of God and His Holy Word you will become a spiritual slob.

If you are not spiritually working out with God you are weak in God. You might know a few things about Him, but you don't know Him. It's huge to know that God's Word is sufficient. You may believe it's infallible, but do you know it's enough to live on? I read this Tweet from one of my favorite preachers the other day...

The modern church is producing passionate people with empty heads who love the Jesus they don't know very well.
-Voddie Baucham

Look once again at Philippians 2. It's such a fantastic chapter. Look in particular at this passage again:

Therefore, my beloved, as you have always obeyed, so now, not only as in my presence but much more in my absence, **work out your own salvation with fear and trembling,** *for it is God who works in you, both to will and to work for his good pleasure.* -Philippians 2:12-13

I started lifting weights and working out at around age seventeen. Back then, in the 1980's, there was the rise of these massive fitness gyms that provided everything. They had showers, locker rooms, saunas, steam rooms, ice plunge, and towel service... and the cost was exorbitant. You had to sign the contract, etc. And you had to make a fashion statement with spandex, legwarmers, and headbands. I couldn't do that. So I went the opposite way.

I joined the grungiest, most tattered gym in the city. I lived in Fort Worth, Texas, and in the industrial section of town there was a dirty gym set up in an old warehouse. The name of the place was Balloons. There were no contracts. There was some huge dude at the front door that took your money. You didn't have a nice little laminated card to swipe. He knew your face. You paid by the month and they gave you a flimsy receipt that they printed on the computer in their back room. The big dogs trained in this gym, and it was old school. It was the training center for those who were in competition or who were serious about lifting weights. It was definitely not a gym filled with soccer moms who were looking for a place to go to get a smoothie after a few reps on a machine or two.

They never talked about it, but I suspected you were expected to fit in by taking human growth hormones. One day in particular I remember walking in and this gigantic Schwarzenegger looking dude had a syringe in his hand, shooting up a woman in the hip. I had to scoot by them to get through the door. I guess you could say they took steroids, lifted weights, and ballooned up.

I also found one of these grunge-type gyms in Florida when I lived there. It was fantastic. There was no dressing room at this place and it, too, was rough. You felt tough in there and if you didn't, you were in trouble. Those dudes who came in there were huge, and they all rode motorcycles. You could feel there was something suspicious about the place.

A few years ago, Missie and I were watching a late-night documentary on television about motorcycle gangs and they showed this rough, tough, mean gang outside of Orlando, in Apopka, Florida. They showed their hangout— a gym. Wait a minute! I sat up in bed and looked with my mouth agape. It was that gym! That's where I worked out!

Here's the deal: there is authenticity and there are fakes. There are genuine believers and there are frauds. There is real and there is bogus. There are those who are serious and those who just want to put on a show. There are those who play around and those who get down to business. In the Christian life if you are serious, and earnest about seeking joy, you will seek to work out your faith in Christ. And I have found that those who are resolutely honest get into a routine. Paul is telling the church at Philippi some interesting things. They are things that transfer easily to us, living in the twenty-first century.

1. Paul says, "I am not there... act like I am"

It's easy-peasy to act like a Christian when we are around Christians. It's simple to live godly on Sunday mornings. I don't mean to sound facetious, but I'll let you in on how to be a fake Christian: You just nod your head when someone is pouring their hearts out to you. You say "Amen" a lot. You say "brother" or "sister" as you respond to their cries. And oh, here's the best one— you tell them you are going to pray for them when they corner you after the worship service. You do that so that you can get away from them and out the door so you can go eat lunch.

The real Christian life is one of integrity. In other words, it is who you are when no one is looking. Fake Christian joy will make you neither happy nor satisfied. Question: If you say you are going to pray for someone, do you do it? Even when you have a ballgame to watch? Even when you promised your mate you would let Netflix entertain you for the evening?

Paul is telling the church at Philippi, basically, "I may or may not be coming back to see you." He says later in this same chapter, "I'm sending Timothy to you... and I hope to come see you myself." Paul may or may not be there to encourage his fellow believers, but he is urging them to grow up regardless. God is looking for us to mature in Him. He desires that we live right, righteous, God-fearing lives.

Here's an example from my lifelong interest in working out. I know how to lift weights. I know the correct form and technique. I also hate— I mean hate— working out with someone else because I am usually in a hurry to get it done, and I don't like to talk while in the gym. Just my preference. But, also, at my age I don't want some young guy telling me what to do in weightlifting. I've been lifting longer than those guys have been alive, I tell myself.

So, about a year ago I was lifting and this young dude looked at me and said, "Old man, you're doing it wrong." I said, "Shut up!" Well, not in so many words. He was bigger than me and he really didn't call me an old man. I asked him to help me— I was just being nice— but he was right! He knew what he was talking about! I got more extension on this one triceps exercise, and it helped me immensely.

As the pastor, I'm not around all of the time to help keep church members and my brothers and sisters in line as they follow Jesus. Your mom is not around all of the time. Your Christian spiritual guru that you listen to on television

62

or the Internet is not around all of the time. But God is. And Paul is saying upfront, "I— the one who founded the church, the one who led you to Christ and taught you about Jesus, the one writing the letter to the Philippians, the one you depend on to be there— am not there." And he didn't need to be.

One of the best things you can do today is to realize that Jesus is enough for you. You may have a church— you need one— and you may have Christian friends, but walking with Him by yourself, and the Holy Spirit walking with you, may just be all you get in this life. You and His Holy Word may be all you have to go on, so count yourself blessed. I used to be envious of others who had famous Christians, or a plethora of godly people, around them. But I now know this: The Word of God and the Holy Spirit walking with you, illuminating His Word to you, is all you need. And for most of us, it is all we are going to get.

2. When you work out you need to exert faith energy

Don't get confused by this verse. Paul says, "work out your salvation with fear and trembling." Salvation here is not referring to your *justification*— meaning your forgiveness in Christ that results in your eternal life and place in heaven. It sounds like Paul is talking about your rescue by God, but he is not. Your salvation is not contingent on you knocking on doors or meeting a quota. You cannot work your way into the good graces of God to get to walk the streets of gold. No, God puts faith in us. The technical term is *monergistic*, meaning *God does it*. It's alien to us. It comes from outside of us. God puts faith in us! We don't possess faith prior to God saving us. God does the rescuing.

The key technical term you absolutely need to know as we look at this verse in Philippians is *synergistic*. Do you know that word? It comes from the word *synergy*. It's you and someone else combined to get the job done. It's now you and God... or God and you. Paul is saying now that you are a Christian you have skin in the game, start working out your Christian life. He rescued you, so seek Him daily and repent regularly. Believe me, we can't lose our salvation. If we could then we would. Think about that statement a few minutes.

It's your duty to grow yourself. You don't have an excuse. Do you own a Bible? That's all you need most of the time. You need a church, you need Christian brothers and sisters, and you need to see and hear the Word lived out in front of you. But if you never get those things, you can get it all from God's Holy Word.

I learned how to lift weights the correct way forty years ago. I learned to work out a section of muscles, and then let those muscles regroup and rest and work out another set of muscles. Now, since I've disciplined myself to study God's Word regularly and to seek Him in prayer, when I read Scripture the routine and truths of God seem to jump off of the pages and work out my heart so that it gets stronger. My faith and trust in God is sound and solid. Now I can face anything the enemy throws at me— with God.

Let me give you a workout routine. All athletes and in-shape people need workout routines. Here's one that is sure to bolster your soul. Last week, as I read through my daily Psalms reading (I read through the Psalms 6-7 times a year, with a pen and marker in my hand), this one made me spiritually stronger. I was looking at Psalm 69 and when I got to verses 16-18...WHAM! It was like I lifted a new world record! Here's what it says:

Answer me, O Lord,
for your steadfast love is good;
 according to your abundant mercy,
turn to me.
Hide not your face from your servant,
 for I am in distress;
make haste to answer me.
Draw near to my soul, redeem me;
 ransom me because of my enemies!
                                    -Psalm 69:16-18

The Psalmist is begging for an answer from God. He wasn't in a hurry to pray and get it over with. He was determined, and knew that only God could answer Him. Then we see that he knows God has a steadfast love and a lot, that is, a *lot* of mercy. So he says, "God turn to me." He's experienced what we all have: "God where are you? I'm hurting God, please, please, now, now, answer me." Again, it's "God come near." Then there is that word *redeem*. Redeem is related to money. It means to buy back. So this what I said, echoing the Psalmist, "God, I've run off from you and I've become a slave to someone else. This old world. It's trapped me and has made me its slave. God buy me back! God rescue me, ransom me." It looks like he has realized that everyone else but God is his enemy. Folks, that's a faith work out. Try it. It gives you strength, both spiritual and emotional.

3. Your workout is for God

Admit it, anyone who works out learns to look in the mirror. Why do we call mirrors *vanities*? Because we are vain! When I was eighteen or nineteen, I wore out the mirrors in our house. I posed, I flexed. I did the Hulk Hogan. I copied and mimicked Frank Zane's and Lee Haney's Mr. Olympia poses. My two younger sisters, Cheryl and Laura,

65

laughed and called me conceited. The more they complained, the more I flexed.

Beware: in your God workouts the spiritual muscles you build are surely for flexing and posing, but not for yourself or others. God demands righteous living, but for whom? Not for you and me. Read the Psalms, read the Word of God and you will find our right living and holiness is for Him. God created us for Himself, not we for ourselves. You and I have flabby spiritual muscles when we think we are so super-spiritual that our religion makes us proud. Pride is flabby fat, not Christian muscle. Pride does not make us joyful. As a matter of fact, it's just the opposite. It will make us envious of what others have and, when that happens, joy goes out the window.

If you pay attention you will see a faux-Christian attitude constant among immature Christ followers. Let's look at a scenario: Rather than making a fantastic witness in a restaurant, the flabby Christian puts on a show when the server asks if they want something from the bar. Instead of "No thank you" comes the curt and boastful, "I don't drink!" As if the server really cares. Why don't we engage in conversation to plant a seed about Jesus at this point, or at least invite them to church? You never know how they may respond. Here are a few more examples of spiritual flab:

- ⮑ You and I have flabby spiritual muscles when we measure our closeness to God by how we don't cuss or smoke or drink.
- ⮑ You and I have flabby spiritual muscles when we think we are better than our neighbor who doesn't go to church.
- ⮑ You and I have flabby spiritual muscles when we think God loves us more because we say "Hallelujah" or speak Christianese.

⮕ You and I have flabby spiritual muscles when we meet someone who is not a Christ follower and our opinion of them is that they are a loser.

⮕ You and I have flabby spiritual muscles when we tell someone we will pray for them, but never do.

⮕ You and I have flabby spiritual muscles when we say we have read the Bible, but in reality it is thick with dust.

⮕ You and I have flabby spiritual muscles when we preach of giving to those in need at Christmas, or giving to a charity, while never tithing to our home church.

⮕ You and I have flabby spiritual muscles when we correct others with "Don't judge," when we never invite anyone to Christ or to church. We've already judged them hopeless.

You've been raised on the Message of the faith and have followed sound teaching. Now pass on this counsel to the followers of Jesus there, and you'll be a good servant of Jesus. Stay clear of silly stories that get dressed up as religion. Exercise daily in God—no spiritual flabbiness, please! Workouts in the gymnasium are useful, but a disciplined life in God is far more so, making you fit both today and forever. You can count on this. Take it to heart. This is why we've thrown ourselves into this venture so totally. We're banking on the living God, Savior of all men and women, especially believers. -1 Timothy 4:6-10

The Baylor Bears men's basketball team won the 2021 NCAA tournament. I smirked as I read about the team's motto for their championship season: *Culture of JOY.* Coach Scott Drew's brilliant, God-instituted theme is the formula for winning. *X's and O's* are drawn on the whiteboard before the game and half-time for roundball strategy, but putting Jesus first, others (teammates) second, and yourself third is the real recipe for a victorious life. Joy is not only the game plan for Baylor basketball, but it is their goal too. Here's the lesson: Get a tactical plan for building spiritual muscle!

What does it cost to work out with God? Is it free? His salvation is free to us, the gym membership is free, but working it out, growing strong in Christ, will cost you something. You don't have enough money in your checking account to buy your way into God's good graces or into heaven. If you won the Powerball jackpot tomorrow, you wouldn't have enough. If you had the money of Bill Gates, Jeff Bezos, and Mark Zuckerberg combined, you wouldn't have enough to get into God's gym. You see, it cost Him the life of His Son, and He gives us His grace. He supplies our faith to us, and wants us to join Him in order to grow it.

The down payment was when they falsely accused Him, and beat Him. The first payment was when they pressed a crown of thorns down onto His head. They stole from our Lord, taking out more payments by blows, and then the final payment was due. They nailed the spikes into His hands and into His feet. They pierced His side. And when they couldn't take anything else from Him, the workout payment for you and me was complete. It was finished.

Joy is that we get to join His gym for free. And that joy grows exponentially when we workout our spiritual selves to grow in Christ— when we strive to know Him and His will for our lives. It is pure joy to know God, and to know that He knows you. If you are looking for one of those plush workout gyms where they have big screens and modern equipment to make you think you are working out your faith, then don't bother with this passage of Scripture in Philippians. You would hate to know the number of weak churchgoers who have walked down an aisle, while the people were singing some soft music, and who repeated a prayer but never passed from death to life. If you want to build spiritual muscles God's way, then it will cost you everything. Sign up today, give Him your life, and you will finally go from being weak to being strong.

Chapter 5 – **JOY123** Study Guide:

J1 Can you recall if you have ever trembled, sensing the presence of God in any situation? It may just be where you need to be, to experience the joy of **JESUS** in your life. Working out your salvation means having a plan for spiritual growth. I challenge you to write out, in one paragraph or less, a plan to meet God every day. We plan meetings, work, vacations, games, and leisure. But so often we fail to plan an hour with God, or half-hour, or even just ten minutes. Make those minutes count. You will tremble in His presence before you know it!

_____
_____
_____
_____
_____
_____
_____
_____

02 Recently, my friend was conducting a funeral for a family member and he looked so calm and collected in a difficult time, and I remarked how well he did. He replied back to me, *"We were all trembling."* Think and pray for **OTHERS**. Make a point to pray for preachers and teachers as they stand before the people and proclaim the Gospel. If they are sincere and true to God, they realize the gravity of the message of Jesus Christ, and tremble before Him. Craft that prayer right here:

_____

_____

_____

_____

_____

_____

_____

_____

_____

Y3 Looking in the mirror after a workout is a common egoistic thing in our culture. When **YOU** work out with God, what features are you gazing at in the mirror? Begin to take notice of your strength in love, hope, peace, and patience. Count the times you are kind, and look for the gentleness and goodness in your life. Are these things there or are they missing? And by all means, count the joy because it is when you feel the strongest.

_____

_____

_____

_____

_____

_____

_____

Chapter 6

Complaining is Cussin'

Do everything without grumbling or disputing....   *-Philippians 2:14*

Mrs. Hester Haynes, a widow, was my babysitter in the late 1960's. I bestow and deem upon her the title of Best Babysitter the World Has Ever Seen. Born in 1899, she was a sweet, kind Christian woman. She had twenty-three dogs that ran around outside her shack of a house that was probably built around the same time she was born. We were allowed to run and play outside and in the woods, and pick strawberries from her garden. When she cooked lunch for us, we would sometimes have spaghetti, but she didn't prepare a sauce. She put ketchup on top of it! I always thought it was gross. My sister and I had the best time at Mrs. Haynes', but one thing you did not do was *cuss*. Several times I saw her wash her grandson's mouth out with soap! Once I put a little soap on my tongue to test it out, and I quickly decided the ketchup was just fine.

This has to be the message of all modern messages for our critical world. I don't need to read your emails, your texts, your snail mail, or listen in on your phone conversations to conclude that most everyone has a problem with complaining. You may think I've been eavesdropping on all of your conversations with your buddies, or that I've been over in the corner at Starbucks or Waffle House as you have been talking to your bestie. I haven't. It just looks that way. But I know exactly what is going on in your life. I've seen the grimacing expressions on your face and the grouchy attitude towards communication.

Going further in Philippians, still in chapter two, we turn to this single command from God to you and me. It leads right to the Good News of the Gospel and how we are supposed to live. Yet the bad news is most of us will smirk, smile, admit our guilt, and then go out and live like we never heard God say it. Here it is again:

> *Do everything without grumbling or disputing....* *-Philippians 2:14*

Whoa! Where did that come from? Upon first glance, most of us would settle for people doing some things without grumbling, disputing, or complaining.

> *Do everything without grumbling or arguing....* *(NIV)*

> *Do all things without murmurings and disputings.* *(KJV)*

> *Do everything without complaining and arguing....* *(NLT)*

> *Do everything readily and cheerfully – no bickering, no second-guessings allowed!* *(The Message)*

Everything? Wouldn't this also be in the first chapter of the socialist manifesto? "Put on the uniform, everybody is treated the same, and do everything without grumbling and complaining." Maybe so, but God is not a cosmic malevolent dictator. He is not into us conforming. No, He is the God of transformation in Christ. Change is the name of the game in the Christian life. And we do it for true joy.

Questioning the establishment is good for democracy. It may be good to have a press corps to interrogate the president and politicians. We are allowed to complain peacefully about DoorDash forgetting the special sauce for our sandwich. Every now and then we can grumble with our spouse about life being difficult (maybe). Murmur and mumble about how your neighbor waters their yard 24/7 and lets their dog use your yard. Go ahead and engage in irenic argument with the opposition, or those who are against your reasoning that Clemson is going to win the National Championship next year. Dispute the calls at the basketball game by yelling to the referee that he is a zebra. Do all of that. But when it comes to obeying God, folks, there is no statute for standing in opposition to Him or disagreeing with Him.

Let's keep going. Take someone to court to sue them because they have done you wrong if there is no way around it. Call the law when someone is trespassing on your property and won't leave. Write to your Congressman when your rights have been infringed upon. Invite your friend over for a cup of coffee and talk to them about how your former friend did you wrong, and get some advice on how to get past it and forgive them. You are free to do all of that! You and I have rights. You need to stand up for yourself. You need to be a man; you need to be a woman! Go for it. Be a person of justice. But for the love of God, for the absolute love of God, when He tells you to do something,

- Just as partial obedience is an oxymoron; delayed obedience is a contradiction in terms-

Thinking that one day you will obey God or submit to God doesn't make sense. Why do we delay? Simple. We don't want to do it.

> *Do all things without grumbling or disputing, that you may be blameless and innocent, children of God without blemish in the midst of a crooked and twisted generation, among whom you shine as lights in the world, **holding fast to the word of life**, so that in the day of Christ I may be proud that I did not run in vain or labor in vain. Even if I am to be poured out as a drink offering upon the sacrificial offering of your faith, I am glad and rejoice with you all. Likewise you also should be glad and rejoice with me."*
> *-Philippians 2:14-18*

Over 450 years ago, in February of 1555, John Rogers was killed. I know you probably don't know who he was, but he was a great man of God. He was a Bible translator. In the 1500's it was illegal to translate or own a Bible translated into English. Wild isn't it? John Rogers took over translating the Bible after William Tyndale died, and he published the translation they had been working on for years. He went by the pseudonym *Thomas Matthew*. He thought this disguise was good enough, but it wasn't. The Pope caught him in January of 1555, and sentenced him to die. Think about that. The church, and the leader of the church, had the power to kill people back then. Interesting.

They didn't allow Rogers to spend even one more night with his wife. That's the church for you isn't it? Sometimes they eat their own. He was led to the executioner on February fourth. It was a Friday. The French Ambassador said the people gave encouragement to Rogers as he was led, and *"even his children assisted at it, comforting him in such a manner that it seemed as if he had been led to a wedding rather than an execution."* That my friends, is obedience to God.

This is what Paul is saying. "If I am poured out as a drink offering upon the sacrificial offering of your faith, if they kill me right now because of your testimony of obedience, then it's worth it!" This isn't second grade Christianity. This isn't Vacation Bible School with Paul saying, "Okay class, no fighting, no hitting, no throwing your erasers, no getting up without raising your hand, keep your hands to yourself, no grumbling and complaining, or disputing...." No, that's not the deal here at all. Paul is saying, "Don't you get it? It's all about character! It's inner character! It's who you really are in Christ. Focus! Concentrate! Make sure you are walking with Him every day. That means quit complaining about the petty stuff of the world, and start really living." You are a light. This world is dark and twisted. We are called and built to shine in the darkness. Joy comes out of obedience.

Nope, this isn't VBS Christianity, but it is primary. Your attitude, your character in front of others, and your testimony with or without words, counts. If living a godly life— that is, a right life before God— is anything, it is what you can and cannot say. Some turn twenty-one and think that because of their newfound liberty they can talk and curse without ramifications. Not so. If no one has told you yet, then let it be from my mouth: Quit using God's name in vain! If you think what I am saying is too elementary for you, then you just don't get it. Quit peppering expletives in your daily vocabulary for the fun of it. Quit using the F-word, the

S- word, the X-word (I threw that one in for the fun of it). Quit just letting words come out of your mouth and then use the excuse, "that's just who I am." You are more than that if you are in Christ. Don't let obscenities dictate or define who others think you are. Grow up. Perhaps joy escapes your life because others hate the way you talk and don't want to be around you? Jesus says, "It's not what you put in your mouth, but what comes out." In other words, your words reveal your true heart. If Christ hasn't gotten a hold on your tongue maybe the unbridled gateway to your life is blocking your joy.

Think about how, of all the things Paul could have been talking about here, he chose to address how we deal with each other. In chapter 6 of the New Testament book of Acts, in the very first verse, we see that the way they related to each other was causing problems. It was about the day-to-day ministry in the local church in Jerusalem...

> Now in these days when the disciples were increasing in number, a **complaint** by the Hellenists arose against the Hebrews because their widows were being neglected in the daily distribution.
>
> *-Acts 6:1*

Other translations use the words "murmurings" (KJV) and "rumblings" (NIV). God is not going to put up with our attitudes, period. So what good is my telling you about not complaining, about not having bad attitudes, going to do? Where is that going to get you? You really don't need an explanation, if God says it. But Paul tells us why in these few verses of Philippians 2. There are several reasons:

1. To be Blameless

If there is anything I work on in my life these days, this is it. I don't want to be blamed for something trivial. God holds me accountable to my words and my attitude. I work diligently on these things and I beg of you to do the same. Here are some practical Biblical transforming words that come out of this passage in Philippians:

- ➲ Quit talking about people.
- ➲ Quit sending out negative vibes.
- ➲ Grow up in Christ.

You can't have joy in your life if all you do is spout critical words of hate and discouragement. Control over your mouth is definitely one of the signs of growing up as a believer in Christ. Be uplifting and encouraging. It is truly a mark of maturation in Christ. In the next book after Philippians Paul writes to the church at Colossae and, in chapter one, says this:

> To them God chose to make known how great among the Gentiles are the riches of the glory of this mystery, which is Christ in you, the hope of glory. Him we proclaim, warning everyone and teaching everyone with all wisdom, **that we may present everyone mature in Christ.** For this I toil, struggling with all his energy that he powerfully works within me."
> -Colossians 1:27-29

Maturity is the goal. You cannot mature in Christ if you are complaining and arguing and grumbling and murmuring constantly. What is the maturity goal? Here are five synonymous goals:

- ➲ Christ-like
- ➲ Perfection
- ➲ Right living

● Holiness
● Without blemish

Paul says perfection is what we are going for. You say that's impossible, and you are right. Without Jesus it *is* impossible. But with Him, you are not just on your way, you are perfectly righteous in God's eyes.

2. To Shine brightly

Those without Christ live dim and dark lives. Why? Because, as the Bible describes, that's the dark world in which we dwell. The world does not have true light to offer. It has only simulated light. That is, fake light. God calls us to watch our speech because not only do we carry around a reflection of Jesus, but we are actually light in darkness. If you want joy in your life then you need to bring the light, the joy of Jesus, to others.

Do you cuss when the lights go out and you can't find the flashlight? Maybe God shakes His head when we have the opportunity to shine His love before others, but still choose to curse the world. When we have the chance to exhibit a godly manner and attitude, to reflect— and in a sense to refract— God's love from ourselves to someone else, do we let out a string of curse words for others to hear? Try speaking joy and happiness over a foul mouth and see what happens. It will change your life.

There are people who do good work, but they are not real lights. CH Spurgeon said this,

> *If you profess to be a Christian, yet find full satisfaction in worldly pleasures and pursuits, your profession is false.*

Don't just talk about it, live it. And watch for it in others around you. Here's a quick sermon for you: A lot of your stress in this life would end today if you just got rid of so-called friends who are dragging you down with a darkness that you think is light.

> As the truth of Christ is in me, this boasting of mine will not be silenced in the regions of Achaia. And why? Because I do not love you? God knows I do!
> And what I am doing I will continue to do, in order to undermine the claim of those who would like to claim that in their boasted mission they work on the same terms as we do. For such men are false apostles, deceitful workmen, disguising themselves as apostles of Christ. And no wonder, for even Satan disguises himself as an angel of light. So it is no surprise if his servants, also, disguise themselves as servants of righteousness.
> *-2 Corinthians 11:10-15*

3. To hold fast

Everyone needs a tattoo. I'm not talking about the ink on your skin. I'm envisioning a tattoo on your heart. God's Word needs to be inked on your life.

Did you know Jesus has a tattoo? The Bible says that written on His thigh is "King of Kings and Lord of Lords." Read it in Revelation 19. Listen also to what the Bible says, repeatedly, in Psalm 119. The Psalter frequently exhorts us in the 176 verses of that great chapter with repetitive phrases like these:

➲ Make me understand the way of your precepts
➲ I cling to your testimonies, O Lord
➲ Turn my eyes from looking at worthless things
➲ I will keep your law continually

- ➲ My soul longs for your salvation
- ➲ I will never forget your precepts
- ➲ I do not turn aside from your rules
- ➲ I incline my heart to perform your statutes
- ➲ My flesh trembles for fear of you

There are many others. Apply them to your life. Tattoo them on your heart. Go to it first in your life, not last, and go to it early in the morning. Often you hear people that are distressed say, "Well… there's nothing left to do but pray!" Stupid saying. It should be the first thing we do, not the last.

Paul uses a bit of personal testimony and plea at this point. He says, do this for the glory of God and, when I see it, I will know you listened. If I would give a bit of personal testimony, then I would say I haven't seen a lot of grumbling and complaining among the people of FRESH Church. If there has been, then they are good at hiding it. Or it could be that, on the first day of our organization, I made the announcement that if anyone wanted to argue or complain then they could leave. We don't have time to argue in the Kingdom of God, there is too much to do.

We are not going to hold fast, or slow to complaining and moaning. Our fellowship is not going to do it. At the time of this writing, we are trying to build our first building. We have been wandering around from place to place for so long, we just want a home. We are about the business of the Lord, to make disciples, and not about building a structure that other religious people will envy. I would rather have the ugliest building in town— I mean, one so ugly people talk about how stupid it looks— and have a sweet fellowship of Jesus followers, than to have a beautiful building but inside it be empty hope with empty souls, living out empty lives.

4. To Rejoice

Paul couches everything he says in joy. I believe Paul got up and delivered fiery sermons every now and then, but I don't think this is one of them. I think it's simple teaching: just quit moaning, murmuring, cussing, complaining, and arguing.

"So Pastor, why do we do it? How can I stop from doing it?" Here's the answer: *Pray for joy.* Read that statement again: Pray for joy. It's amazing that we will go to God in our prayer life with our list of things for God to grant, like He's Santa Claus. Yet we don't reflect His holiness in the way we talk to Him. We have our happiness planned out and want God to give His approval, rather than trusting Him and asking Him to give us His joy. Pray for joy in your life. Ask God for it.

Charles Spurgeon said this:

> *A heavy wagon was being dragged along a country lane by a team of oxen. The axles groaned and creaked terribly, when the oxen turning around thus addressed the wheels, "Hey there, why do you make so much noise? We bear all the labor, and we — not you — ought to cry out!" Those complain first in our churches who have the least to do.*

You may not be complaining out loud, but I guarantee you that one day, all of those complaints you hold inside will make you just quit. I've seen it. I've seen it in church for the last thirty years. People come, and they sit in the seat, and they wait for that magical Walt Disney World moment— when you see the stars, and you hear the music, and all of the characters are in their places— and they are waiting for the feeling, and when the feeling doesn't come, or when they have had their say of how church should be done, they are out of there.

On the night He was betrayed, He was in the Garden praying and the disciples couldn't pray for even one hour. They fell asleep. But something was going on as Jesus prayed to the Father. He was asking Him if there could be another way. If there was ever any time in the history of the world for anyone to complain or argue their point, it was then. Going to that Cross was going to be painful. It was a torture chamber of torture chambers. It was hideous in pain, insidious in planning for agony. But Jesus, our Lord, didn't complain. He acquiesced to the Father in total obedience. And because He suffered and died on the Cross, you and I can have joy that one day we will see Him face to face.

Inside of twenty to fifty years, most everyone reading this will see Jesus face to face, eye to eye. Either He is coming here or you are going there, it doesn't make a difference. You will see Him, you will stand before Him, and if your name is not in the Lamb's Book of Life, you will be cast into hell. Grumbling and arguing to Him is not going to do you any good. Only submitting and following Him is the way to joy.

Chapter 6 – JOY123 Study Guide:

J1 Please let me direct your attention to the Ten Commandments. Number three on the list deals directly with what we have talked about in chapter 6: *"You shall not take the name of the Lord your God in vain, for the Lord will not hold him guiltless who takes his name in vain."* God was serious about how we treat His name. The name **JESUS** is holy. It is a sign of our maturity in knowing He is Holy. So do a quick inventory on your mouth. What comes out? Do you honor God with your language? What are your biggest complaints? Write them down here and then pray for God to give you a different attitude and vocabulary in dealing with it.

_____
_____
_____
_____

02 OTHERS are in your life because God put them there. You are responsible and accountable for your words spoken to them. Joy, many times, comes from repenting of the way you speak about others. Stay away from curses on others. Think about someone you don't like or maybe someone who doesn't like you. Yes, you love them in Christ, but they rub you the wrong way. Write down at least 10 encouraging words that would describe their best asset and traits. Now, pray those for words for them.

_____
_____
_____
_____
_____

Y3 Listen today for only edifying words. Dismiss negativity and only invite constructive criticism. Learn from others...remember, God put them in your life. What 10 words describe the joyful person God wants **YOU** to become?

_____
_____
_____
_____
_____

Chapter 7

Biting Dogs

Look out for the dogs, look out for the evildoers, look out for those who mutilate the flesh. 		*-Philippians 3:2*

I'm a jogger. I log about seven hundred miles a year. It's a great stress reliever and after years of doing it, it's become habitual. I have a regular jogging route in my neighborhood, and mapped out in my brain are the homes with dogs. A runner has to look out for dogs. A couple of years ago I had the pleasure of being bitten twice in one week by two different canines. One bite was on my heel. A Chihuahua, of course— I once owned a chihuahua, so I know how evil those little devils are. The other bite was on my hip, my behind, by a bigger dog. The bites didn't hurt too bad so I just kept going. Runners really don't like to be interrupted. After my mouth unexplainably started foaming an hour later, and I got a little dizzy and somewhat confused... just joking, my tetanus shot was up to date, and I was only sore. Not long after that I changed my route, but I still hear barking dogs and I usually look to assure they are in a fence or tied up. For my safety, I need to know where they are all located. Here's my advice to runners *and* Christ-followers: Look out for the dogs! Dogs will rob you of your joy.

As we move through chapter three of Philippians the Apostle Paul warns us of mean dogs without leashes... vicious dogs unfenced... wild dogs running loose on the church. These Pit Bulls of Perdition, Dobermans of Deceit, and Rottweilers of Ravage will bite you! Dogs in the New Testament were not pets, they were scavengers. So when the Bible refers to dogs, it doesn't mean Fido or Spot or Shnookums. Their reaction to dogs was more like our own apprehension towards coyotes. Let's look at this big section of Scripture in this letter to the church at Philippi:

> Look out for the dogs, look out for the evildoers, look out for those who mutilate the flesh. For we are the circumcision, who worship by the Spirit of God and glory in Christ Jesus and put no confidence in the flesh—though I myself have reason for confidence in the flesh also. If anyone else thinks he has reason for confidence in the flesh, I have more: circumcised on the eighth day, of the people of Israel, of the tribe of Benjamin, a Hebrew of Hebrews; as to the law, a Pharisee; as to zeal, a persecutor of the church; as to righteousness under the law, blameless. But whatever gain I had, I counted as loss for the sake of Christ. Indeed, I count everything as loss because of the surpassing worth of knowing Christ Jesus my Lord. For his sake I have suffered the loss of all things and count them as rubbish, in order that I may gain Christ and be found in him, not having a righteousness of my own that comes from the law, but that which comes through faith in Christ, _the righteousness from God that_

depends on faith—that I may know him
and the power of his resurrection, and may
share his sufferings, becoming like him in
his death, that by any means possible I
may attain the resurrection from the dead.
-Philippians 3:2-11

Amazingly, I mean, *amazingly*, this letter to the Philippians speaks to us two thousand years later as if it were written yesterday. It's as relevant to our own spiritual lives as if you had received it via email or text this morning. Paul is concerned about the purity of the Gospel. It's about faith and faith alone. He is concerned about others adding something besides faith to the Gospel in order for us to be saved. But no one should add anything to, nor detract from, the Word of God. Even the penultimate verses of the Bible in Revelation 22 caution us of this,

I warn everyone who hears the words
of the prophecy of this book: if anyone adds
to them, God will add to him the plagues
described in this book, and if anyone takes
away from the words of the book of this
prophecy, God will take away his share
in the tree of life and in the holy city, which
are described in this book.

Paul, in the third chapter of Philippians, was talking about the attempt to teach about Jesus *plus* Old Testament ceremonial law. We would call it an add-on in today's world. They wanted to add on circumcision. What is circumcision in spiritual terms? Well, of course, it is the cutting of the male genitalia, but it had significant symbolic meaning in both positive and negative ways.

- ⮞ **Positive:** God is cutting out his people from other tribes. He is separating them from other nations to be a holy people, to be a blessing.
- ⮞ **Negative:** The Jew is saying, "If I fail to keep every one of the terms to the Covenant (Deuteronomy 28) then may I be 'cut off' from your presence. Just as I have cut off my foreskin, may I be cut off from you."

It's easy to see the figurative representation of this sign. Here's what it means to us today: The Cross of Jesus Christ is the supreme circumcision. By putting our sins on Him, He was *cut off* from God. Get it? Read the Gospels and we find God turning His back on His Son because of grotesque sin.

One Sunday, right before I walked up to the podium to speak, my throat was a little dry, and I reached down for some water. The water bottle's seal had been broken. Uh-oh. And there was a little bit of water gone...uh-oh again. Now, this bottle was probably left over from the week before and it was my bottle, but I didn't know that for sure. Would you drink it? You would have to think about it, right? It may not be clean. Yet still we drink in impure Gospel talk every day in our lives, and the kicker is that we don't think about it being all that important. Purity of the Gospel was important to Paul.

Paul called those who wanted to add things to the Gospel *dogs*. That was about as low a name as you could get in those days. In the epistle to the Galatians he was talking about this same subject, and declared that those who add anything to the Gospel should go to hell. Tough talk isn't it?

Fast forward a thousand years from the Cross, and the add-on to faith in Christ included doing everything the Catholic Church said. It wasn't just enough to have faith in Christ, but you also had to take on the traditions of the church. You had to go to the priest for absolution, you had to go to Mass, you had to give money for indulgences to move family members from purgatory to heaven, and you had to kiss the Pope's ring, among other things. These add-ons were elevated to being just as important to salvation as was Jesus dying on the Cross, thus Paul's reference to dogs.

Fast forward another thousand years. Let's say, the latter part of the twentieth century. Just fifty years ago you had to dress a certain way, and wear your hair a particular way, to be accepted in some churches. Those were add-ons. Then things changed, dresses were a little bit shorter, and a little bit shorter, and a little bit shorter... being casual, dressing how you wanted in order to be cool, became the same as adding-on to the Gospel message. We added casual, come as you are— and if you can't come as you are to church then you are not a real church. Do you see how perverted we have made the Gospel? The Gospel of Jesus Christ is purely Him crucified, buried, and raised again. Nothing more, nothing less.

Philippians 3 is huge today because we are living in a church world that is preaching a cheap gospel. Here's the deal: for most people, when they need gas for their car they look for the cheapest gas. They even have an app for it. We love the dollar store, or the superstores like Sam's and Costco, because we are convinced there is savings. But studies show that if you just shop smart, the other stores are competitive in price. When we see the word "sale" we've all become Pavlovian dogs: saliva starts sliding down our chins as we think about 30%, 40%, 50%... oh, could it be? Could it ever be? 90% off? I got tired several years ago of preaching a cheap Gospel. I realized that I was just feeding people what they wanted to eat, and they were getting fat! I don't do it anymore.

As I age and grow in Christ I find that it's not easy to follow Him. We are accustomed to gaining, or adding things into our lives, for happiness. However, real joy comes not necessarily from addition, but more by subtraction. If you are just trying to fit Him into your lifestyle, it doesn't work. As a matter of fact, that is when the pain starts in your life. Coming to church is not like pushing a shopping cart and when we find some grace on this aisle, or faith in the produce section, or love in the bakery, or peace in the meat department, we just throw them into the buggy. Rather, it's throwing yourself on Christ like a helpless person. And here's what I mean:

1. Your Boast will always lead to Burnt Toast

Your boasting will burn you in the end. Did you catch the part where Paul gives his resumé in verses 4-6? It's as if he was saying, "Do you think you have a great curriculum vitae? You think your list of accomplishments is impressive? Ha! Look at mine...."

> ...I have more: circumcised on the eighth day, of the people of Israel, of the tribe of Benjamin, a Hebrew of Hebrews; as to the law, a Pharisee; as to zeal, a persecutor of the church; as to righteousness under the law, blameless.
> -vv 4-6

However, Paul wasn't lording it over them, he was making the point that all our achievements and accomplishments don't impress God to bless us or love us more.

What does "circumcised on the 8th day" mean?

All Jewish male infants were circumcised on the eighth day. It was law. It was in keeping with the covenant made to Abraham in the Old Testament. Isaac was circumcised on

90

the eighth day. Jesus was circumcised on the eighth day. Paul is saying, *"With respect to circumcision, I'm an eighth day-er!"* In all likelihood, most of those "dogs" started out as Gentiles and then came to the "Jewish" God we know. So they were circumcised later but it still counted in their religion or commitment, even though it wasn't on the eighth day of their birth.

Here's what we might hear from the modern-day equivalent of the *eighth day-er.* "I've been a part of this church since the beginning. I'm more important than the Johnny-come-lately. I've been giving longer, praying longer, serving longer, suffering longer, so I'm more spiritual. Look at my pedigree!" Listen, if that is your attitude in service to King Jesus then that boasting will lead to you being charred like burnt toast. I'm talking about overdone. Over and over in Scripture we are taught humility, not superiority. Jesus is the bread of life, not the toast of your boast!

What is "of the people of Israel?" Paul was not of mixed stock. He could trace his family lineage back to Abraham! And not just to Abraham alone, but Abraham, Isaac, and Jacob. It was Jacob whose name, after wrestling with God, God changed to *Israel...* and his descendants would become God's people. The chosen people, or the privileged people, that is.

DNA genetic testing is important to some. It is often a big deal to someone to find out where their ancestors came from. Personally, I don't want to find out I have any more kin! Just kidding...a little. Paul was presenting his DNA report, and it was spectacular. It went right back to Father Abraham and Paul's audience would have said out loud, "Whoa, he's important."

What does "tribe of Benjamin" mean? Paul is taking it up another notch. In America, the claim to fame for

wealthy people used to be millionaire. Not anymore. Now, it's billionaire. For the actor, it's Academy Award status. For musicians, it's nomination to the Rock and Roll Hall of Fame. For Pro football players, it's winning the Super Bowl. Paul mentions the tribe of Benjamin because they were the elite— the aristocracy of Israel. In Judges, when the men of Benjamin went to battle, it says they had seven hundred left-handed soldiers who could sling a stone at a hair and not miss! The first king of Israel was a Benjamite: Paul's namesake, Saul.

What is Hebrew of Hebrews? Here, Paul is saying he is the purest of the pure. Period.

What is "as to law a Pharisee?" *Pharisee* was a position of great honor to the Jews of Paul's time. And with all of those other attributes Paul lists in his resumé— you get the picture.
Paul then says,

> *...The very credentials these people are waving around as something special, I'm tearing up and throwing out with the trash—along with everything else I used to take credit for. And why? Because of Christ. Yes, all the things I once thought were so important are gone from my life. Compared to the high privilege of knowing Christ Jesus as my Master, firsthand, everything I once thought I had going for me is insignificant—dog dung. I've dumped it all in the trash so that I could embrace Christ and be embraced by him...*
> *-vv.7-9 (The Message)*

2. Your Loss leads you to the Cross of Christ

The Gospel of Jesus Christ is not cheap. Here it is. Here's the expensive stuff: You have to count everything as a loss in following Jesus. I'm not writing this to cheat you or hold you back, I'm writing to be honest with you. Unless you give it all up— I'm talking about trust— unless you give it all up to Him, you will never gain Christ. If you want to know God, you have to go to the Cross of Jesus Christ, and the way to get there is to get rid of everything in this world you think makes you *somebody.*

Sports is a competition and so is life. School, politics, and athletics, among many other things, are all competitions. But God isn't a competition. He's not going to share your heart with your wants. *"Pastor Greg, what about my dreams and desires to use my intelligence and my giftedness and my talents?"* You are getting ahead of God with that sort of thinking. For years and years, Christian authors have produced manual after manual on leadership. Maybe there have been great results, but way too many leaders have opted out of a godly life. While we major in leadership, God is talking about Lordship. Who do you live for? What is it that proves you a Christ follower? Can you define that?

> *"...everything I once thought I had going for me is insignificant—dog dung."*   -v.8

The English Standard Version (ESV) translates dung as "rubbish" and the Greek word is σκύβαλον (skubalon). Do you know what that means? Dog...yep...dung. Paul wants to get to the lowest thing on the planet. And don't think I don't know that many of you use the same term, in a different slang, on a regular basis. Measured beside Jesus— unless you see all of your money, all of your diplomas, all of your jobs, all of your awards and accomplishments, all of your so-called self-worth, as σκύβαλον— you cannot gain Christ. Your self-measured self-worth is canine manure when you stack it up next to the Lord Jesus.

The cheap gospel being preached today says you can get rich following Jesus, and that you will always be healthy. Ignoramus preachers say you will always be smiling and happy, and that you will always *feel* like it. They take it further by saying you will get all you ever wanted, and that you will understand everything that happens in this world. We fall for it because it looks so good. Many hear that and confuse it for joy. Those *things* are not joy.

Financial advisors say, "cut your losses." Paul, here, is saying, "cut all of your gains!" Because they are really nothing but losses anyway. The Gospel is as anti-this-world as we can get. It's weird to think of losing, of dying, of giving up our stuff, of being humble, of being subservient, of the first being last and the last first, of sacrifice, of poverty, of meekness, and of pain and suffering, as the things that our God most desires in our lives. Unless we grasp that this is what Paul is doing with his own life, then we just won't get it. Only at the Cross will you discover that all your life's stuff is just a loss.

3. Giving Him Your wrongs leads to long gains in Righteousness & Resurrection

It's misleading to say Christ accepts us the way we are. Rather, He accepts us *despite* the way we are. He receives us only in Christ and for Christ's sake. *How do you know when you have bought cheap grace?* When you haven't changed from who you were. You will best comprehend the true transformation to His image when you've moved on from where you were and are now producing fruit: love, joy, and peace. There is patience in your life. Maybe there is a gentleness and goodness about you that you've noticed. You live to seek kindness and forgiveness. There is self-control others have discerned. You want to know Him more. Yes the old you still wants to hang out, and that's a good thing for measurement's sake, but you don't like that old person. You recognize the old nature, the old you, and you move on! In Christ you are a new you.

> *Even the most mature saint will struggle against worldliness and apathy toward God. There is no sincere Christian who does not lament his or her spiritual & moral failures. Yet this lamenting is one evidence of conversion. The unregenerate (those not saved) are unconcerned about such things.* —Paul Washer

You don't have to be the smartest person in the world to realize you need to change your lifestyle. It's easy math: 2+2=4. Those drugs lead to depression, guilt, and despondency toward life. That adultery and pornography puts distance between you and your spouse, and God, and leads to guilt and destruction. Those friends, those so-called friends that you know you don't need to hang around, aren't going to magically disappear one day. But let me tell you this: if they get *their* lives right, then they will disappear from *your* life because they don't want to be around the likes of you!

What you believe right now is taking you somewhere. Where doesn't matter but, wherever it is, you are going *somewhere* and you are riding on the front bumper of the vehicle. Paul was circumcised on the eighth day and was of the people of Israel, of the tribe of Benjamin, a Hebrew of Hebrews, a Pharisee— and all of that was leading him to arrest and torture those Christ-followers of the first century. But then change came about in his life. That beam of light in Acts 9? Yes, it was Jesus. I find it interesting that

Paul didn't head back home. Instead he continued on to Damascus, and there his eyes were opened. He discovered the change that had come about in his life.

What's the message? It is this: Giving Him your wrongs leads you forward to right living. Long for it, because it is the only thing that matters. Wherever you go in this life, the dogs are going to be barking. They are trying to get out so they can bite you and terrify you. Change your route, go God's direction. He will lead you forward to the beautiful change He wants in your life, and you will look more like Him. The less you have of this world, and the more you have of Him, the more joy you will have.

Chapter 7 – JOY123 Study Guide:

J1 If you want some joy today, then boast in the Lord **JESUS**. Read Psalm 30 and discover when the joy comes. Meditate on it and find out how God turns things around in our lives. Study it and find out how many times, in different ways, the Psalter tells us to worship. Then write them down:

_____
_____
_____
_____
_____
_____
_____
_____
_____
_____
_____

_____

_____

_____

_____

02 Recount your worst loss in life. Did you lose a family member? Did you lose a friend? Were **OTHERS** considered in your tragedy? How did God make it so that all things worked together for good and joy came out of it? Describe in a few sentences how He did it:

_____

_____

_____

_____

_____

_____

_____

_____

_____

_____

_____

Y3 In Philippians the Apostle Paul is building, in **YOU**, joy for a lifetime. Too often, we are looking for a "shot" of joy to tide us over until we get paid, or get past a bad time. God is all about transforming your life of doubt, criticism, and pain, to one that has total security and hope in the Lord Jesus. Pick a Psalm passage on joy and memorize it. Psalm 30:5; Psalm 35:27; Psalm 51:12; Psalm 66:1; Psalm 95:1; Psalm 126:5; or pick one of your own from the 50+ verses of joy in Psalms.

Chapter 8

The Goal

Not that I have already obtained this or am already perfect, but I press on to make it my own, because Christ Jesus has made me his own.

-Philippians 3:12

Goal-oriented people get it! If you define a goal clearly, then they will pave the road to get there. "We are at point A, and I need you to get to point B." Just move aside. Don't worry about them, they will find the way. Goal driven folks get up early, map out the plan, and then get going. Maybe not every goal-oriented person is a high achiever, but then again, maybe they are. And then there is everyone else. Several simple scenarios surmise my point on goals:

➲ In 2014, in Flint, Michigan, there was a crisis and, from my understanding, it is still severe. Do you remember it? Inadequate treatment of the water supply caused a contamination of the water. Many of those affected got sick and experienced terrible skin conditions. What would you think would be the goal in fixing this problem? Of course, the answer is to purify the water. But, years later, politics is the issue and the water is still not pure.

➲ If someone breaks the law by robbing a store or assaulting someone, what should happen to that person? They are now criminals, so they should be arrested and brought to trial. If convicted, they should pay the penalty. What is the goal? Justice. You have to make a wrong into a right. It is very necessary to make things right.

➲ A big game is coming up and your basketball team has days, or perhaps weeks, to prepare and get ready. What is the goal? It's not personal statistics, or to be a hot dog. It's not for the victory party afterwards. It's to win the game. In any ballgame, the goal is to win. And we are told that winners practice harder and smarter, and are more focused. Practice is about getting it right.

➲ You enroll in college to further your education. You study hard and make good grades. What is the goal? To graduate with a degree. The staggering statistic of college students who graduate in four years, compared to the number enrolled, is 33.3%. That means two-thirds are not reaching the goal.

What is the goal of this life? Have you ever thought about it like that? I know you have goals at work, and you have goals at school. A smart parent develops goals for their family. If you are thinking about retirement, then you have financial goals to meet before the big day.

What is the goal of the Christian life? It's right living. Period. The Bible calls us to be holy, and to live a righteous life. The word *holy* appears more than six hundred times in the Bible; the word *righteous,* over five hundred. *Holy* means to be set apart and sacred, whereas *righteousness* is just a fancy word for right living. Christians are set apart from the world by living right. Can the Christian life be any simpler?

Maybe you remember what the Apostle Paul said in Romans— that the righteous will live by faith. What does that mean? So many think the goal is heaven. "If I just make it to heaven (fill in the blank)." The result is they confuse salvation in Christ with having to do a bunch of good deeds in order to get into the good graces of God, or to get to that desired place. The bad news is that good deeds will not save you. There are people who are simply hoping they will make it, as if there's a 50/50 chance. That is the exact opposite of joyful living. Thinking that the goal is more and more church, or more and more religious good-stuff, will wear you out and disillusion you. Good things are good, but they are not the goal. Some think that the goal is more Bible knowledge, so that one day you will figure out what is going on. But knowledge is not the goal. What about spiritual gifts...is that the goal? No. What about looking and being nice and happy, and kind— surely that is part of the goal? No.

The goal is living right, and that means being obedient to God and His commands. Righteousness has to be the goal because the Bible says it is. Over and over in Scripture we are called, admonished, and warned— yes, *warned.* "Our God is a Holy God, He is without sin." In Leviticus 11, it says, *"Be Holy as I am Holy."* And all the way to the end of the Bible in the New Testament, Peter echoes those same words,

> *As obedient children, do not be conformed to the passions of your former ignorance, but as he who called you is holy, you also be holy in all your conduct, since it is written, "You shall be holy, for I am holy."*
> *-1 Peter 1:14-16*

Adam and Eve were hurled out of the Garden of Eden because of their unrighteousness. Holiness is serious business to our God. Levitical law (the book of Leviticus) painstakingly takes us through the rituals and sacrificial system, for what? To rid sin, to clean us up, to be made right before God again. Righteousness must be the goal because Jesus, God's Son, was without sin and He showed us how to live a holy/righteous life.

Righteousness is the goal of life because Jesus says,

> *For I tell you, unless your righteousness exceeds that of the scribes and Pharisees, you will never enter the kingdom of heaven.* – Matthew 5:20

Righteousness must be the goal, because it's all Paul talks about! Righteousness has to be the goal of life because God cannot look upon sin, Habakkuk tells us so. Righteousness has to be the goal of life because the Bible says that everyone has sinned and fallen woefully short of God and therefore cannot please God. Everyone has let God down. Sin has put distance— a lot of distance— between us and God. Jesus is the bridge to that distance. He walked into this world and John the Baptizer looked and said, "Behold the Lamb of God, the One that takes away the sin of the world!" Yep, it's righteousness all right. Goals are pretty clear in life, so why is there so much failure? There is a connection between going for the goal of living right, and joy.

Why do we lack so much joy in the Christian life? Why is there so much disappointment in a God-centered life? If right living is the goal, then why this fiasco of disobedience on our part? Why this debacle of duty and submission? Why wrong living? The easy word is sin, and it would be true. But let me interpret it and make it even more clear for you: we don't value what God values. Often we describe sin as dark, hidden things in our lives. In reality, sin can be good things that we have elevated above God. It all goes back to that first commandment, *"Don't have any gods before Me."* Many don't think God's Word adds any importance for us, so they disregard it. For the most part, this world does not believe in going to church, meeting with the family of God, and the result is contrary to joy. It's a miserable life. Most don't have confidence in a God out there, in our personal lives, intrinsic or transcendent. We would rather post some platitudes on our social media pages about how much we believe in Jesus. But if we were to follow a great number of people around for twenty-four hours and see the dirty, rotten, nasty lives lived out before a holy and righteous God, we would be sick to our stomachs.

I have called this chapter "The Goal," and this passage in Philippians is a fantastic verse to study and commit to memory:

> *Not that I have already obtained this or am already perfect, but I press on to make it my own, because Christ Jesus has made me his own. Brothers, I do not consider that I have made it my own. But one thing I do: forgetting what lies behind and straining forward to what lies ahead, I press on toward the goal for the prize of the upward call of God in Christ Jesus.*
> *-Philippians 3:12-14*

Here's what Paul is declaring: *I'm not a fully mature Christian yet.* Those are revealing words from this great Christian ambassador. We surely have to like this statement because it means there's hope for you and me. When we think of the Apostle Paul we regard him as the greatest Christian to ever live. General knowledge and assumption about Paul is that he was light years ahead of us in knowing God. Why? Because he not only saw Him, but he walked with Him and talked with Him. We would assume that a person this smart would pity us, and our interpretation would be that he is obligated to God to reach back to us and say, "C'mon, you low down people, you losers, you good for nothings, come on and try to keep up with me here." However, that's far from the truth. What Paul is doing here, in chapter 3, is being real with us. He is not getting technical, or religious, or even puffed up. He is not getting above our heads or talking in philosophical terms about God. Nor is his theology over our heads. We just need to take the time to understand it. He says two things about following God that we should tattoo on our brains and etch in our hearts. For us, as believers, we need to realize this is not just surface talk. It goes deep. Remember, if you want to go deep with God, you have to go further with God. I consider these two points massive to us as Christians as we grasp our solidification, our foundation, in salvation.

TWO Massive Points For reaching THE GOAL OF RIGHTEOUSNESS

1. Forget the Past if you have been Forgiven the Past

Paul starts like this: "*But one thing I do....*" In order to live right, you have to forget the past life of sin. It's difficult because many times that guilt of iniquity lingers on our minds. What kind of God would He be if He said you are forgiven... "but I'm going to file away in the back of my mind all the times you flipped me off, and if you mess up again, I'm going to research my files and bring all of those past things you did wrong back out, and I'm going to torture you, punish you, and sentence you to the full extent of your wrongs!" You can't serve a god like that. You would never know when you are right with Him if that were the case.

But maybe that is our problem? We just don't know the magnitude to which we have been forgiven. This little religion game that most people are playing is getting to them. When we look back, we uncover an enormous misunderstanding of forgiveness. Reflecting back, remembering, contemplating, trying to figure out why the past still haunts us, shows that we don't truly understand and grasp the totality of forgiveness of Jesus or, ultimately, His suffering on the Cross.

Roger Bannister was the first man to run the mile in under four minutes. 3:59.4 was his time. It was an August day in 1954. But Bannister really wasn't the best runner that day. John Landy led most of the race. He was on a record pace. Bannister was running in second and for some reason Landy, as they neared the finish line, looked back, and that look back caused a split second of wasted motion in his legs. You wouldn't think that nanosecond of turning his head would result in such a huge mess-up. But it was enough. Roger Bannister was right there, and flew by him. Nobody really remembers Landy, and Bannister is in the record books forever for being the first to break the record. Landy broke Bannister's record by 1.4 seconds a month later... but who cares? Landy said, *"If I hadn't looked back, I would have won."*

This is exactly what Paul is saying. You've been forgiven of that horrid, disgusting, and grotesque sin, so don't look back. Don't go there my friend. Don't you realize the colossal impact, the completeness, the entirety and broadness of the forgiveness of Jesus Christ? Could that be it? Could that be why you have stalled out in your Christian life? Maybe you don't realize you are saved, and rescued to the uttermost! Yet you are— you are totally free in Christ. Joy comes in knowing this.

"But one thing I do" means a focused concentration on Paul's part. It is a mental obliteration of the course which a runner has already covered. Quit racing against, or comparing yourself to, other people or other Christians. Compare yourself to Christ. He is perfect and He calls you and me to live a perfect, right life. Landy thought he was racing Bannister. But no, he was racing the track. And just like on the racetrack, on the track of life there is no looking back.

There is a big, yet terrifying illustration of this in the Old Testament. God tells Lot to get out of Sodom and Gomorrah. Run! Run for your lives. Yes, you can take your wife; yes, you can take your kids; yes, you can take your in-laws...but run! Get out as quickly as you can. And here's the interesting part: Lot just dragged his feet. He was making excuses and seemed lost in space, just like we do many times when God says to run from sin and to run to Him.

On my last trip to the Holy Land we stopped off for a moment near the Dead Sea, and our guide pointed to the giant salt pillar on the edge of the range. It's the figure of a woman, frozen. It's the image of Lot's wife. What happened? She looked back. The Bible says she then immediately turned to salt. It's a reminder that there is nothing for us to look back to.

God subsequently destroyed Sodom and Gomorrah. Was Lot's wife looking back and thinking, "I wish I had stayed, maybe I could have made a difference." Or, was she saying, "I sure miss my friends. Maybe one day they will change?" It's what we do. Many times we hesitate like Lot, and look back like his wife, and we miss God's righteousness. It's the point where many of our spiritual lives break down. It's where many Christ-followers are stalled, frozen in time. Too many so-called Christians are looking back and dreaming of those old, empty days. There is one incredible verse that is huge here. It's just three words and it's the third shortest verse in the Bible, behind 1 Thessalonians 5:16, "Rejoice always," and the shortest, John 11:35, "Jesus wept." The verse is this:

> *Remember Lot's wife.*
> *-Luke 17:32*

This passage of Scripture is some of the best teaching you will ever get. Let me repeat it: *remember Lot's wife.* Looking back, she not only froze but she missed the goal of life— to glorify God. Let me put it another way that should get your attention if you are a Christ follower: Looking back on sin is forbidden by God. Why does God forbid it? Because He has put it out of His incredible mind. If you don't know Psalm 103:12, then you are going to be blessed after you read this about Him and how He works:

> *For as high as the heavens are above the*
> *earth,*
> *So great is his steadfast love toward*
> *those who fear him;*
> *as far as the east is from the west,*
> *so far does he remove our*
> *transgressions from us.*
> *-Psalm 103:11-12*

God chooses not to remember our repentant sin. Some preachers will put it like this: "You need to lay your sin down at the Cross." Since Jesus died for your sins, then you commit to follow Him, turn from your sins, and leave them at the Cross of Christ to die! If you have been forgiven the past, then forget about it. Leave it behind.

2. Press on w/ Passion for the Goal: The Purpose of the Prize

Paul's statement, *"Press on,"* means to surge ahead. Joy never comes from looking back. Again, don't do it. Rather, rush ahead with Christ. There is a graphical picture of a runner straining to reach-out-as-far-as-he-can-to-get-to-that-finish-line. It's not a stroll. It's not nonchalant. It's not one of those races where you say, "I'm going to walk part of the way." No. It's all out. Life is difficult for you and me. Right living is tough but, Paul says, strain to do it. He urges, "I know you want to take a break from it and relax and get some Gatorade, but you can't. The race isn't over!"

Here's the sad picture of the Christian life for so many: You signed up for the big race. You got all suited up in your running attire, you bought the Nike Zoom Pegasus Turbo 2, or the Under Armour HOVR Phantom 2, or whatever your favorite running shoe. You exercised. You went to the training events. You ate all of the right stuff leading up to the race, consuming the right amount of carbs and proteins. You bought the tickets to get there, traveling hundreds of miles, and then you walked into the colosseum or stadium. You gazed at the track, and observed how perfect it is for running. You saw all the aid workers and officials there to help you make your run perfect and fun. The stands for Gatorade were lined up on the running route. They assigned you a race number and you stuck it to your chest. You gazed at the starter. You walked up close to the starting line. But then instead of putting your foot down on the track you wedged and weaved your way up through the stands and sat down in the upper deck between some regular fans, to watch everyone else run.

Yes, it's easy to make fun of the slowpokes. It's easy to make fun of the loud and funky clothes they choose to wear. It's easy to cheer on the best-conditioned athlete and applaud the G.O.A.T. (*Greatest Of All Time*). But you should be on the field. You should be on the track. You should be running the race of life and when you fall down, you should get back up. When you catch yourself moping, limping, or falling behind, you remember Coach Paul calling out, *"Keep straining toward the goal!"* When you get winded, or your mental and spiritual muscles ache, you remember your training. You knew it was going to be difficult. So keep going! The suffering is not a surprise to the mature Christ-follower, it's expected.

Paul is presenting to us a passion for running the race of life. Don't lose your passion for Jesus. The way to achieve that is to keep seeking Him in His Word, on your knees, and with the body of believers called the church. The way is the mission, and fulfilling the Great Commission. Keep doing this, and joy will follow. You were called to the race by the head running coach Himself, Jesus. If you keep going then you will always be on the starting line and in the race. Keep running the race, and joy will follow.

The prize for those ancient Olympic games in Greece was a green wreath of leaves for you to wear on your head, five hundred drachmae, free food at all the restaurants, and front row tickets to a Greek tragedy at the theatre. That's a pretty good package deal. A drachma was a day's pay, and now showing at the original Caesar's Palace: *Oedipus Rex* by Sophocles. Not only do we, as Christ-followers, not realize the massive forgiveness in Christ on the Cross for our sins. Most of us don't realize that the prize of salvation in Christ is handed out *before* the race. Who does that? Who hands out the prize before the race?

Here's the deal: You are not even in the stadium, and God comes and puts you in the arena of life, on the track of realness, with the correct spiritual attire, and says, "Run."

And so many of us say, "I don't know how! I'm too old." And God says, "Cool... then walk."

> *We were buried therefore with him by baptism into death, in order that, just as Christ was raised from the dead by the glory of the Father, we too might **walk** in newness of life.*   *-Romans 6:4*

> *...in order that the righteous requirement of the law might be fulfilled in us, who **walk** not according to the flesh but according to the Spirit.*   *-Romans 8:4*

> *...for we **walk** by faith, not by sight.*
>   *-2 Corinthians 5:7*

- ⮑ Run this difficult race.
- ⮑ Walk with Jesus every day.
- ⮑ But whatever you do, don't sit down.
- ⮑ Whatever you do, don't quit.
- ⮑ And my goodness, for the love of God...don't look back!

What is the prize? It's that completion of righteousness. There is something deep down in you. Everyone has it. You want to be right with God. You may have suppressed it to the point that you don't think about it, but we all want to be clean, pure, right. I'm begging you to understand this during your pursuit of joy in this miserable world. John Chrysostom, the noted ancient church preacher, says that the pursuer of a goal...

> *...sees nothing, he thrusts away all who impede him with great force, he cherishes his mind, his eye, his strength,*

his soul and his body, looking at nothing other than the crown.

It doesn't say so but I wonder if Paul smirked, thinking about those Olympic prizes, as he wrote of the goal. I wonder if, in a cloud above his head as he wrote, he was envisioning the Olympic prize package. That money? That VIP ticket to the theatre? If he did, then he would think it nothing compared to the riches Christ. I wonder if he scratched his head when he thought about that prize of eating free at any restaurant in town. Eat free hummus and pita bread? Are you joking? With our God we will be eating at the supper table of the Lamb in all glory!

And then, think about that little leafy wreath they put on your head to crown you. Paul wrote to Timothy, "An athlete is not crowned unless he competes according to the rules." Those without Christ are competing for a leafy crown that will soon wilt and die. But when we press on, forgetting what is behind us and straining forward to what is ahead... Jesus says,

> *Be faithful unto death, and I will give*
> *you the crown of life.*   *-Revelation 2:10*

Perhaps you have been looking for a goal worth getting into the race for? You have found one today, it's the crown of life – Jesus! That's why Paul refers to it as joy.

➲

111

Chapter 8 – JOY123 Study Guide:

01 Let's play word association! write down the first thing that comes to your mind for each of these words. Your answer can be any length.

- ➲ JESUS
- ➲ Righteousness
- ➲ Sin
- ➲ Salvation
- ➲ Mission
- ➲ Discipline
- ➲ Church
- ➲ Serve
- ➲ Bible
- ➲ Give
- ➲ Holy Spirit
- ➲ Heaven

_____

_____

_____

_____

_____

_____

_____

_____

_____

02 Joy 101: Forgive **OTHERS**. Let's just tackle it head on. Write down the names of the people that you hold a grudge against, or who hold a grudge against you. Pray this incredible prayer:

"God, bless and protect and be good to my enemy! Give them opportunity to grow and flourish and give to your Kingdom. God, I can't forgive them, but you can because you live in me. Strengthen them to be successful and good to others. In Jesus name, Amen."

Was that tough? Do it again tomorrow if you are serious about having joy in your life!

_____

_____

_____

_____

_____

_____

_____

_____

Y3 Psalm 4 says, "You have put more joy in my heart than they have when their grain and wine abound." As **YOU** pray for God to put passionate joy in your heart, list the things you are passionate about in this life. Try to describe or define what makes you passionate for them. Can you have a passion for God? If you do then joy becomes clearer and clearer.

_____

_____

_____

_____

_____

_____

_____

_____

_____

Chapter 9

Citizenship

I remember one of the first times I flew out of the country, over three decades ago. On my return, coming down that tunnel in the airport leading to the security check-in and customs, I saw a poster of the President. It said, "Welcome home." I don't know about you, but I like to be welcomed home. No one wants to be gone for a while and, after all the weary and exhausting travel, you walk in the door and someone just says, "Hey." No, we want fanfare, congratulations, or a ticker tape... and then we want to go to bed. If you are an American citizen, have you ever read your passport? It has writing in there. They're very important words. It's the very reason for the passport. Here's what it says:

> *The Secretary of State of the United States of America hereby requests all whom it may concern to permit the citizen of the United States named herein to pass without delay or hindrance and in case of need to give all lawful aid and protections.*

It's a document securing a certain privilege of safety and security.

I am a proponent of bringing back Civics as a mandatory class in public schools. It's a good thing that some of us are born as citizens, because I don't think we could pass the test to become a national of the United States. It's a difficult test. Look it up online. The process is called naturalization. If you are a naturalized citizen of the United States then you weren't born here, but you moved here, followed the laws, and took and passed that test. Here are the naturalization requirements:

- At least eighteen years old.
- A lawful permanent resident of the United States for at least five years before applying for naturalization.
- Physically present in the United States for at least five years at the time of application.
- Able to understand and speak English.
- Of good moral character.
- Complete Form N-400, Application for Naturalization.
- Get two photographs of yourself that meet immigration service requirements (pose, size, lighting, etc.).
- Collect the necessary documents.
- Send your application, documents, and filing fees to the appropriate Service Center.
- Receive an appointment letter from USCIS.
- Go to the fingerprint location and get your fingerprints taken.
- Mail additional documents, if requested.
- Receive an appointment for your interview.
- Go to your local office at the specified time.
- Bring identification.
- Answer questions about your application and your background.
- Take the English and civics tests.
- Receive a ceremony date.
- Check in at the ceremony.

➲ Return your Permanent Resident Card.
➲ Answer questions about what you've been doing since your interview.
➲ Take the oath of allegiance.

Could you do it? Here's my conclusion: thank God I was born on U.S. soil, making me a citizen with all the rights ordained and given to me by the constitution of the United States of America.

Are you a citizen of heaven? It is where Paul wants to take you and me.

> *Brothers, join in imitating me, and keep your eyes on those who walk according to the <u>example</u> you have in us. For many, of whom I have often told you and now tell you even with tears, walk as <u>enemies</u> of the cross of Christ. Their <u>end</u> is destruction, their god is their belly, and they glory in their shame, with minds set on <u>earthly</u> things. <u>But our citizenship is in heaven</u>, and from it we await a Savior, the Lord Jesus Christ, who will transform our lowly body to be like his glorious body, by the power that <u>enables</u> him even to subject all things to himself.*
> *-Philippians 3:17-21*

These are tremendous words to close out chapter 3 of Philippians. Joy is written all over it. The Good News is that those in Christ have been naturalized. We are no longer citizens to speak of this world, but citizens of another world— heaven. It's funky sounding, but for those in Christ, there is a flight you will be taking one day, there is a spiritual threshold you will be crossing.

Just this morning a friend, Jerry, a dear saint in the Lord, died of COVID-19. I only met him less than a year ago. He was one of five men in my father-in-law's Sunday School class who had died from the virus. An older man, Jerry gave his retirement years traveling with a band of joyful brothers, going from town to town a few times a year to do missionary work. His last project was to come and help me. He was a gentle big man. His job in helping my church construct our building was to run the saw. The time of death was 3:33am. Jerry was ready to go and be with the Lord he loved so. His bride had died of cancer several years ago. When I talked to his close friend, he said to me, "Brother Greg, down here in our part of Alabama, we have the old red hymnal... and number 333 is 'I'll Fly Away'." Jerry went home to glory.

> *My heart is in anguish within me;*
> *   the terrors of death have fallen upon*
> *me.*
> *Fear and trembling come upon me,*
> *   and horror overwhelms me.*
> *And I say, "Oh, that I had wings like a dove!*
> *   I would fly away and be at rest;*
> *yes, I would wander far away...."*
> *   -Psalm 55:4-6*

If you are in Christ, your passport has been stamped in advance and, really, you are already in line or sitting in the terminal... waiting for your flight to be called. You will fly away one day. You have first class seats, TSA Pre-check, you don't need any luggage, and baggage isn't allowed. This is joyful news. This passage of Holy Scripture in Philippians 3 is to be celebrated in your life and mine. It tells us that there is more to this life than just 80-100 years on this planet, than that little in between dash ("-") on the tombstone, and your family eating potato salad and a Chick-fil-A party tray after your funeral.

My favorite workout guru encourages, "Don't attach yourself to the outcome, but enjoy the journey." That's great advice for those that are putting their faith in their bodies to be shaped and sculpted when they are 150 years old (like it will happen), but it's terrible advice for the Christian. We have to look at heaven in order to endure the journey! Walking through this life to have joy, without Christ, is impossible. Here's what Paul is saying about it.

TWO Different Styles of Walk…

1. Clearly: Follow MY Example (Paul says)

Whoa! What happened to Paul's humility? When a preacher or teacher these days says, "act like me and do what I tell you to do," we get panicky and start thinking 'cult,' and maybe we should. But Paul is not going Jim Jones on them and demanding they drink the Kool-Aid. He knows they need something concrete, and need fundamental direction. The Gospel and Christian living was new to those early church folk. They may have even asked Paul to describe what the everyday Christian does and looks like. Paul is saying, "follow me as I follow Him." It's not the only time we are told to *imitate* other Christians and Christian leaders in the Bible:

> *Be imitators of me, as I am of Christ.*
> *-1 Corinthians 11:1*

> *Remember your leaders, those who spoke to you the word of God. Consider the outcome of their way of life, and imitate their faith.   -Hebrews 13:7*

119

Beloved, do not imitate evil but imitate good. Whoever does good is from God; whoever does evil has not seen God.
-3 John v.11

Oscar Wilde once said, "Imitation is the sincerest form of flattery." George Bernard Shaw said, "It's also the sincerest form of learning." Imitation may be a curse word in the modern age. We like originality and creativity. There are many things of imitation I loathe. I don't like imitation leather, and I don't like imitation crabmeat. I don't like faux furniture with faux wood. But I love "imitation Paul." Why? Because I can trust him. I can trust him because of where he places his trust: in Christ. He says, "Imitate me, as I imitate Christ." Watch out who you follow and quote these days. It was the same two thousand years ago. Here's one way you should imitate Paul and those early Christ followers (It's how they distinguished real from fake):

The Practice of Giving

That's right. Nothing tells more about you than your practice of giving. It defines you. We are never more like God than when we give. And let me add two pieces of information on how to give:

Eagerly & Often

The popular philosophy embraced these days is just to 'love' others and everything will be all right. Just love. Love people. All you have to do is to love people. Words are...well, what did the little bird say when he flew over J.C. Penney? Cheap, cheap. That silly elementary school joke is awkward, isn't it? But so is thinking that a discounted, bargain, trumped up 'feeling' is love. If love is anything, it is action. Joy in the Christian life is *doing*. Your doing and giving don't save you, and they don't get you to heaven. But they, not your emotions, surely are a reflection of genuine love.

> *When James and Cephas and John, who seemed to be pillars, perceived the grace that was given to me, they gave the right hand of fellowship to Barnabas and me, that we should go to the Gentiles and they to the circumcised. Only, they asked us to remember the poor, the very thing I was eager to do.* -Galatians 2:9,10

Isn't it amazing how you can turn on TV preachers today and they will tell *you* to give to *them*? Here, Paul says, *I* am eager to give! And, and— wait for it— he is eager to do it often. The key to success is to give first. This sounds funky, but before you give away or spend, or buy anything, give to God from every paycheck, stock, or cash gift you receive. It's what my wife and I have taught our son. Give to God first and you will never be unhappy. Maybe there has been a study done, but I've never heard of anyone who sought to give, and give away their lives and their money, who was without joy. Never. Paul says to follow him and his style. Follow him, and how he loved people, into the Kingdom. Follow and walk like Paul and you can't go wrong. Joy will flow, I promise and guarantee it. Continually, throughout the New Testament, you see Paul getting closer to God as he was getting closer to the end. He knew his citizenship was in heaven. Do you?

2. Warning: Watch out for the walk of the Enemy

Do you have enemies? Jesus says, "Love your enemies." God doesn't want us to pronounce judgment on people. He's talking about not pre-judging them, but Scripture also warns us about letting them influence you.

121

Here's our difficult dilemma today: most of us don't know what an enemy of God looks like. The proverbial "red-suited, pitchfork wielding devil" is what we usually look for, but without satisfaction. Misinformed and underdeveloped believers and Christ-followers imagine that the enemies of the Cross, as Paul calls them, are the atheists and agnostics. We believe the enemies of the Cross are mass-murderers, serial rapists, and child molesters. We believe enemies of the Cross are those who take out full-page ads on Social Media in support of some religion in India or Vietnam. That's not what Paul had in mind here at all. Look what Jude says,

> *Beloved, although I was very eager to write to you about our common salvation, I found it necessary to write appealing to you to contend for the faith that was once for all delivered to the saints. For certain people have crept in unnoticed who long ago were designated for this condemnation, ungodly people, who pervert the grace of our God into sensuality and deny our only Master and Lord, Jesus Christ.*   *-Jude 3,4*

In other words, we are looking for the enemies of the Cross to come in the front door, announced, so we can set up guard against them when, actually, they are already sitting right beside you. They could be riding or walking with you. Satan's insidious and diabolical plan has always been to creep. Go back to the Garden, and we find a snake that slithers, or *creeps*. So, if he is the master of disguises, how do we recognize him? Paul was graphic. Look at it:

...their god is their belly, and they glory in their shame, with minds set on earthly things.

The result is that...

➲ **We are Full of Ourselves** – The Greek word for belly is κοιλία (koilia), and it is actually the word for any organ in your abdomen. It's your inner self. It's who you really are on the inside. You see, on the outside you can fake people out but, Jesus says, it's not what you put into your body, but what comes out of it, that is defiled. It's from what's already in there – that jaded heart.

➲ **We are Proud of Shame** – You see, once in this world we all knew what sin was, we called it by name, and we ran from it. But the time has arrived when people use it as their calling card. When you are not ashamed of your behavior, of wronging someone, or mistreating someone, you can bank on it. You are traveling without a passport to God.

➲ **We Focus on Stuff** – The opposite of give is take. Paul zeroes in on our attention to earthly things. To take is to concentrate on collecting more of the stuff of this world in the hope it will make you happy. But Joy will never be achieved by things.

TWO Different Styles of End...

1. Ruin – It is courtesy of a fabricated god

There is no better theology than this: What you believe about God in your life is leading you somewhere. There are only two different roads. There are only two different paths. There are only two different walks. One leads to God, and the other doesn't. One leads to destruction and the other to perfection. One leads to the end of the rope and to ruin. The other leads to the beginning of your hope— which is where joy is— eternity with King Jesus. Destruction and collapse come impolitely and unmannered when you choose to walk away from God. A wrecked life is the result of a counterfeit spiritual lifestyle.

2. Citizenship – It is courtesy of Christ

Paul says, "we wait." It is found 133 times in the Bible, including twenty-three times in the Psalms.

> *Wait for the Lord; be strong, and let your heart take courage; **wait** for the Lord!*
> *-Psalm 27:14*
> *Be strong, and let your heart take courage, all you who **wait** for the Lord!*
> *-Psalm 31:24*

> *I **wait**ed patiently for the Lord; he inclined to me and heard my cry.*
> *-Psalm 40:1*

How long do I wait? One or two days is all you have to wait. That's it? Maybe three. Before you think I've lost my mind...

> *But do not overlook this one fact, beloved, that with the Lord one day is as a thousand years, and a thousand years as one day. The Lord is not slow to fulfill his promise as some count slowness, but is patient toward you, not wishing that any should perish, but that all should reach repentance.*   *-2 Peter 3:8,9*

Just wait a day or two with the Lord. Why? Because He is waiting on you to live a right life. Two roads, two destinations, but there is only...

One Power to Change

> *But our citizenship is in heaven, and from it we await a Savior, the Lord Jesus Christ, who will <u>transform</u> our lowly body to be like his glorious body, by the power that <u>enables</u> him even to subject all things to himself.*   *-Philippians 3:21*

The key words: *transform* and *enable*. You cannot do it alone. He wants to change you, but you cannot change yourself. He will give you the power, you cannot manufacture it yourself. Joy is all about change. Jesus changes you, but you have to turn around and go the other way. That is the basis for repentance. Jesus doesn't negotiate with you about what you can keep. You can't keep anything. You have to be willing to throw it all away and turn to Him. And to give it all to Him. Did you get that last line in verse 21? "...to subject all things to Himself."

The movie, *The Blind Side*, won an Academy Award for Sandra Bullock as Leigh Ann Tuohy, the "adopted" mother of Michael Oher. Oher was virtually abandoned by his parents and experienced a homeless, dysfunctional,

125

inner-city upbringing. He went on to star in football at Ole Miss and was drafted into the NFL, playing for several teams as offensive tackle. He was 6'4" and weighed over 300lbs. The story goes that as Mike was walking in shorts and a t-shirt one cold November morning, the Tuohys drove past him and Leigh Ann said to her husband, "Turn around." Those two words changed the lives of everyone involved.

Those same two words are the words the Gospels preach to you and me about God in a relationship with Christ Jesus. In order to discover the joy of the eternal citizenship in heaven, we first need to turn around. Turn from imitating society, Hollywood, the NBA, D.C., or Twitter, and follow Jesus only.

Chapter 9 – JOY123 Study Guide:

J1 Do you imitate **JESUS** or imitate the world? Think about it:

- ➲ Would Jesus hang out where you hang out?
- ➲ Would Jesus eat what you eat?
- ➲ Would Jesus drink what you drink?
- ➲ Would Jesus dress the way you dress?
- ➲ Would Jesus talk the way you talk?
- ➲ Would Jesus drive the way you drive?
- ➲ Would Jesus walk the way you walk in your spiritual life?
- ➲ Would it be enough for Jesus to spend the amount of time you spend with God?
- ➲ Would what you make be enough for Jesus to live on?

- ➲ Would what you give be what Jesus would give?
- ➲ Would the amount of time serving others be the amount of time Jesus would spend on serving?

02 I am committed to writing ten journals of words to my son, Jackson, before Jesus comes for me. I may make it, I may not. Recently, writing in #3, I wrote to Jackie, "Son, just like there are givers and takers in this world, there are those who seize the day and those who avoid it... be one who seizes opportunity and be proactive." I promise you joy will not come in your life by sitting back and waiting for a handout.

Put your hands to work with the Lord by changing the citizenship of people. Write down the names of **OTHERS** around you who need to come to Christ, and if you can't share with them in person about the love and forgiveness of Christ then write them a note and mail it. Here are the things to include:

- ➲ Your love for them
- ➲ Your prayer for them
- ➲ God's love for them
- ➲ God's plan for them...to come to Christ

_____
_____
_____
_____
_____
_____
_____
_____

Y3 In the 1985 movie, *Brewster's Millions*, the plot is for Montgomery Brewster, played by Richard Pryor, to give away $30 million in 30 days. He's not allowed to own anything or destroy the money, he just has to give it away, and he can't tell anyone what he is doing. For fun, imagine **YOU** had $30 million today, and you have 30 hours to give it away. **YOU** can't tell anyone you are giving it away or why. Where do **YOU** give? Do **YOU** give to God's glory and His causes?

_____
_____
_____
_____
_____
_____
_____
_____
_____
_____

Now pray for wisdom and boldness to give to God.

Chapter 10

Joy Realized

If you are living the Christian life, and you don't have joy, then you are living it wrong. Joy is the hallmark of living for God in Christ Jesus. Paul marks joy as a fruit of the Spirit rather than singling it out as something analogous to an emotional experience. If going to hang out with God's people at God's church on God's Day has become burdensome for you, then you don't understand the fullness of the Gospel. If you serve or give begrudgingly, I am not saying you are not a Christian, but, something is definitely wrong. If you don't pray or have a desire to seek and know the Almighty, you've received bad preaching and teaching somewhere, and you have a massive problem.

Conversely, I am not saying that all of life is one big religious party. Should we laugh, smile, and celebrate continuously? When tough times come and bad times rain down, we are desperate to know where to go. The Psalter says in Psalm 62, "You are my Rock, my salvation; You are my Fortress, I shall not be shaken." You need to know spiritual growth and health sometimes come in seasons. Beware of the thorns, disregard the weeds, and look forward to the harvest. If you have fallen out of love with Jesus (is that even possible?), or never were in love with Him, or you just don't get it anymore, then this chapter is for you.

Philippians is about Christian joy. Our God is a God of judgment and wrath. I also believe He is a God of righteousness and holiness, and I surely believe He is a God that wants us to enjoy life to the fullest. We have to realize we live in a fallen world, and so it's going to be tough. This old world wants to choke us out of life. Of course there is a line to walk. However, we are to seek Him, and when we seek Him we will find Him, and when we find Him we will find joy in living. It is that simple.

In another short letter in the New Testament, Galatians, chapter 4, Paul is dealing with a people in the region of Galatia. They were living without joy. He literally says to them, "I don't get it! I don't know why you started believing the way you do." And that is indicative of many believers and Christ-followers in today's mundane world. Why do we believe untrue things about God? It will only cause us to lose joy. It will cause us to be sad, and perplexed about God. For some it is just eating us alive and we have contemplated quitting. And here is how we quit God these days, without quitting the religious façade:

- ➲ **We quit gathering** with other Christians, but we say we believe in church.
- ➲ **We quit serving**, but we post on social media advocating ministry to the poor.
- ➲ **We quit praying**, but we still hope that one day everything will just work out.
- ➲ **We quit giving**, but we believe the government should give out more money.
- ➲ **We quit reading** God's Word, yet we complain because we can't hear God.
- ➲ **We quit singing** the joys of Jesus, but we can tell you all about the song.
- ➲ **We quit seeking** God, and we get quiet whenever someone mentions Him.

⮑ **We quit living** the joyful life, because we forgot how.

Then, once we quit, let the worst of the worst happen— like losing a job, not having enough money to feed the kids, or someone close to us dying— and we will start crying out to God. Many have quit Him, but let something bad happen and they will tell you otherwise.

More joy is the subject of this chapter. There has to be more or we will die. So many in the church need joy, being miserable due to the dictates of the daily grind. The Christian life is not like a burdensome chore that children try to avoid. Rather it is a carousel of joy where you keep riding with glee, looking for the next go-around. Paul lifts us up by lifting Christ up.

> *Rejoice in the Lord always; again I will say, rejoice. Let your reasonableness be known to everyone. The Lord is at hand; do not be anxious about anything, but in everything by prayer and supplication with thanksgiving let your requests be made known to God. And the peace of God, which surpasses all understanding, will guard your hearts and your minds in Christ Jesus.*
> *-Philippians 4:4-6*

There was a fellow who was about to jump from a bridge. An alert police officer slowly and methodically moved toward him, talking with him the whole time. When the officer got within inches of the man he said, "Surely nothing could be bad enough for you to take your life. Tell me about it. C'mon, talk to me." The would-be jumper told how his wife had left him, how his business had gone bankrupt, and how his friends had deserted him. He had gained weight, and he felt bad every day. Everything in life had lost meaning. For thirty minutes he told the sad story— then they *both* jumped.

Despair is contagious, but so is joy. Joy is God letting us walk and talk with Him. He *lets* us. Despite all the things the world will prevent us from doing, our God lets us hang out with Him every day. Speaking of *let us*, let me tell you my funniest story about lettuce (as if I have more than one):

A man working in the produce department was asked by a lady if she could buy half a head of lettuce. He replied, "Half a head? Are you serious? God grows these in whole heads and that's how we sell them!"

"You mean," she persisted, "that after all the years I've shopped here, you won't sell me half-a-head of lettuce?"

"Look," he said, "If you like I'll ask the manager."

She indicated that would be appreciated, so the young man marched to the front of the store.

"You won't believe this, but there's a lame-brained idiot of a lady back there who wants to know if she can buy half-a-head of lettuce."

He noticed the manager gesturing, and turned around to see the lady standing behind him, obviously having followed him to the front of the store.

"And this nice lady was wondering if she could buy the other half" he concluded.

Later in the day the manager cornered the young man and said, "That was the finest example of thinking on your feet I've ever seen! Where did you learn that?"

"I grew up in Grand Rapids, and if you know anything about Grand Rapids, you know that it's known for its great hockey teams and its ugly women."

The manager's face flushed, and he interrupted, "My wife is from Grand Rapids!"

"And which hockey team did she play for?"

Okay for real, I call this my little lettuce (let us) chapter on joy.

Let Us Be Joyful

Paul says it plainly, "Let's be joyful." Here's a normal daily conversation of what our lives are full of these days:

"How was your week?"

The answer that follows is, "I've had the toughest week. I've had the hardest week. I've had a week from... (and you know what that means)."

Everybody has had a difficult week. Everybody! Some are more complicated and challenging than others, but the plaintiveness and normal calamities persist for us all. We need to learn to deal with them. In reality, the people who are complaining think they don't have enough lettuce—enough dough, enough cash, or enough money, that is. And what they really need is not more money, or more favor, or more stuff to crowd into their lives to create some false sense of happiness. Instead they need more joy, real joy. Here's the kicker: Paul says it twice because, at first glance and first hearing, we could skip over it. It's a command from a saint of God. And the charge is to choose joy.

If your life today is sad or bad, you're mad, and there is no glad in your circumstances, then choose to be joyful. It's a must. Sure, the common response is, "Well, you just don't know how bad I have it." And that's what this passage is about.

Paul is in jail while he is writing. The conditions were deplorable. Do you think he's enjoying shrimp and grits, lying in a hammock, listening to the gentle sound of the breeze on the salty ocean? Do you think he's sleeping on a Select Comfort bed? No! He doesn't even have a Goody powder to dull the headache. I chuckle to think of friends sitting on their back porches in the early hours of the day, reading their Bibles and daily devotion, sipping their lattés and eating their Danish pastry, wondering why the heathen has difficulty with God. Do you think Paul woke every morning in the dank prison cell with a stack of Christian resources to read through while eating his cheese omelet (no ham allowed in the Jewish diet)? Of course not. He was in a tough position for a sixty-something year old man.

It's an enormous piece of lettuce in this chapter. Some are searching and wondering, how do I grow up a little bit more in Christ? How do I become a little more mature in my walk with Jesus? Here it is: *Let us* **choose to be joyful.** Today is filled with many choices, and most of them are going to be challenging. Don't make a bad choice by thinking everything will just work out for the good, if you don't love Jesus. Paul knew the weary condition of followers at that time, and God knows your troubles today. If your joy is stemming from what you have in your garage, then it is not real joy. If your joy and happiness come from a potential promotion, from the way your friends make you feel, or from your Saturday night entertainment, then, unfortunately, you have no clue what joy is. If you think your joy comes by way of the next fashion to be introduced on the red carpet, then you are far removed from joy. But you don't have to be. Let us choose joy.

This is joy: No matter the difficulties, no matter the pain you have suffered, no matter the bad decisions you have made, no matter the hurt you experience, He forgives

134

those who turn away from sin and turn to Him. He has sent His Son for you and died for you, and you are free from it! That's joy— live in it! You are free from the control of sin, the world, and the enemy. That's something to choose to be joyful about. You are not controlled by sin, but instead are free to serve the true God.

Let Us Be Compassionate

There's this strange line that follows Paul's command for us to be joyful. Look at it: *"Let your reasonableness be known to everyone."*

This is a statement on gentleness and fairness. It's a proclamation of empathy. He's talking about real love for people— *Real Love*. Heed these words, because this is how it usually goes with most of us: if you are nice to me then I am nice to you. And if people are not nice to us, we split. What Paul is pointing out is that, as believers, we need to exhibit joy even when others don't. Everyone has someone they wish they could change. Here's how to do it: show joy in your life and they will want it too. Compassion is admired and needs to be copied by Christians.

There's the old story about Mother Teresa welcoming a traveler to her orphan mission in Calcutta. He was a donor come to see the ministry up close. As he walked around and observed the compassionate nun at work cradling and loving the unwanted children, many who were diseased, he said, "I wouldn't do this for a million dollars!" Instantly Mother Teresa, hands deep in care for those children, responded, "I wouldn't either." Money doesn't control everything. Real love is shown in compassion for the least wanted and, every time, joy flows from the love shown.

Let Us Be Calm

No word is wasted in the verses of Philippians 4. Paul says, *"The Lord is at hand."* It means He is coming soon! Then Paul says, *"Don't be anxious for anything."*

135

I like good memes. I saw this one not too long ago:

Sometimes God closes a door. That's it. He just closes it.

Let us, then, be calm and deal with it.

In our anxiety and stress we continue to push for our way, and that leads to unrest and more stress— the very opposite of calm. Jesus was always calm. Calm is a major component of joy. The smarty pants would say, "What about the time when Jesus cleaned out the temple with a whip, He wasn't calm then, was He? It looks like He flew off the handle." Yeah, He did cause a ruckus, but did you notice that verse beforehand? In John 2:15? It says Jesus weaved a whip out of leather. Do you know how long that takes? He was calm and collected and very calculated in what He did. It took more than a few seconds to weave that leather whip, I guarantee it. When the disciples were out on the boat in the middle of the Galilee sea and the waves were whipping the boat around, they thought they were going to die. Jesus was asleep. They woke Him up, panicked, and Jesus says simply, "Peace, be still." Immediately the waves were calmed. Calm comes from calm.

That story illustrates our powerful God and, at the same time, is very real to you and me as we live in the storms of life. We have a God that will either calm the storm or remind us He is in it with us. It should be second nature to us to get up, get dressed, eat breakfast, have our coffee, and get ready for the storm. And when the storm comes, let the peace of Jesus flood your soul rather than letting the rain flood your basement. If you do this, calm will breed calm.

Let Us Plead

...but in everything by prayer and supplication with thanksgiving let your requests be made known to God.

Supplication is another word for an urgent, heart-felt petition. Jesus tells this cool story on prayer saying, "Which one of you has a friend who comes begging for 3 loaves of bread at midnight?" Let's put it in ultra-modern-day terms: It's the wee hours of the morning, everyone is asleep, and your phone rings. Your friend down the street has some rowdy company, they want some pizza, and the pizza delivery service is closed. You've got four frozen pizzas in the freezer but the kids are asleep, your bark-all-the-time dog has settled down, and you are snug and warm. So you say, "Can't," and hang up. He texts and texts and texts until the buzzing of your mobile phone causes it to vibrate right off the nightstand. Finally you text back, "Okay, just leave me alone. Come get them! I'll put them on the porch."

You know pleading is very difficult for some, especially for those who don't like to bow on their knees before Him. It's a pride thing. We think we should be able to ask, "God meet my needs. Amen." This verse blows that thinking out of the water. God has blessed us, and the strange truth is He wants to spend time with us, so we should spend time with Him.

Ask. Seek. Knock. Beg. Plead. Beseech.

➲

Jesus says this about that man whose friend keeps knocking:

> *For everyone who asks receives, and the one who seeks finds, and to the one who knocks it will be opened.*   -Luke 11:10

Then, to make sure we understand that the story isn't about badgering and bothering, Jesus adds this statement describing God,

> *Don't bargain with God. Be direct. Ask for what you need. This is not a cat-and-mouse, hide-and-seek game we're in. If your little boy asks for a serving of fish, do you scare him with a live snake on his plate? If your little girl asks for an egg, do you trick her with a spider? As bad as you are, you wouldn't think of such a thing— you're at least decent to your own children. And don't you think the Father who conceived you in love will give the Holy Spirit when you ask him?   -Luke 11:10-13*

These words should be great joy for us. God is not going to say "Okay, just quit bothering me!" Just as you would not look at your child, your son or daughter who is hungry and asking for chicken nuggets, and say, "You want some nuggets do you? Well, here they are," while shoving them into his face. You don't do that. Or maybe your little girl wants some scrambled eggs. You aren't going to scream, "Scrambled? Are you kidding me? I will boil them and you will eat them like everybody else!" Any loving, kind, and compassionate parent needs to show love and patience with their children. Children are still learning, and need to learn how to communicate properly and respectfully. Jesus says to us, His children, "God doesn't treat you like that."

Your supplication and pleading has little to do with your attitude toward God, and more to do with your desire just to hang out with Him and talk. And that's where joy emerges and blossoms!

Let Us Be Peaceful

I don't know what you specifically pray for in this life, but let me decode for you most of your prayer. You say you pray for your health, but what you really want is peace and solitude instead of chaos. You say you pray for money, but it's really that you don't want to be hounded by debt collectors or to have to scramble to make ends meet. It's really about peace. You say you pray that God will rid the world of war. What for? Peace. You say you pray for a day off, why? Peace. You say you pray for your friends. What do you pray for your friends? They are struggling, sick, directionless. It all points to peace. Peace is a component of joy that is often overlooked. When you find peace, you will be on track and joy will not be far behind.

The anti-war movement of the 1960s-1970s was brought about by war, unrest, and the desire to know freedom...it was really a revolution of peace. Presently, the world is heating up and getting amped up politically, and it looks like there could be nuclear arms problems on the horizon with a few countries. Also new on the scene is climate control, because it appears the world is heating up and causing more problems with the earth's crust, and if we don't get a hold on it then, uh-oh— tsunamis, tornadoes, and tragedy. It's all about peace. Your life may be in turmoil today, and what I offer you is the answer to all your problems...peace. When you have peace, then you have joy.

I have said these things to you, that in me you may have peace. In the world you will have tribulation. But take heart; I have overcome the world.   *-John 16:33*

139

Could it really be that peace is what's missing in your life? Not millions, not job security, and not retirement, but peace. Really? As Paul tells the church at Philippi, God's peace is so perfect for your life that you will not even understand it in its entirety. You need it, Paul says, because it guards our hearts and our minds. I believe you need peace. Why? Because you leave your hearts unguarded when you don't seek Him for it. If you think that you can just say one prayer, or make a one-time commitment, and count on it to take you through decades of turmoil and unrest in this world, it's no different than if you put a million dollars in cash under your mattress and then advertise it on Facebook. It's just a matter of time before someone comes for it.

Without the Holy Spirit guarding your heart, there will be unrest. There will be no peace, and there will be no joy. God chose you, why not choose His joy by rejoicing in Him and seeking Him every day? Don't quit. Eat some "let us" and rejoice!

Chapter 10 – **JOY123** Study Guide:

J1 Look back over your life and write down the experiences for which you rejoiced the most. Was God in the center of those times of joy? Did you recognize God moving and working? Was **JESUS** first in those situations? If not, it's not too late to go back and thank Him for ordering and planning those special times. Write out how and why you thank Him now for those occasions:

_____

_____

_____

_____

_____

_____

_____

_____

_____

_____

02 I've made no secret about what I believe is as close to a spiritual and Christian formula as you can find in Scripture: Jesus first, Others second, and You and me third. It's a natural thing to plead God's love and power on ourselves, but have you pled God's mercy and tremendous blessings on others? Spend some time today truly putting **OTHERS** and their needs above yourself in prayer. Pray for **OTHERS** with the same intensity and sincerity as you pray for your own needs.

Y3 In Philippians 4:4, Paul says, "Let me say it again." Why does he have to say it again? Because we need to be reminded constantly to seek and have joy. We are constantly bombarded by sin and the agenda of this world. If **YOU** could just eradicate those things that hinder you and your walk with Jesus— get rid of them— what would they be? List them:

_____

_____

_____

_____

_____

_____

_____

_____

Chapter 11

Not What You Think

People sold toilet paper for $45/roll at the start of the 2020 COVID crisis. Hand sanitizer prices were inflated through the roof. There was a scare that there wouldn't be enough masks, hospital beds, ventilators, or medicine. They shuttered schools, universities, and sports for several seasons. It was chaos. What could you do? More importantly, what was the church's response? First of all, the posture of the church should be one of running *toward* the hurt instead of running away. If things are cancelled in our culture, sitting by is not an option. When disaster strikes, the church sees it as a fantastic opportunity to love hurting people with the Gospel. The church is called to act, and we need to act to heal. Healing is the essence of Jesus' message. Jesus has healed our broken and sinful hearts and that, my friend, is the core of joy.

He came into the world to give life, to forgive, and not to condemn. Who isn't joyful that once they were lost, and now they are found? Aren't you elated when once you were sick, and now you are well? As Christians, our fear should be the fear of God, and being obedient to Him. Not fear of the enemy, man, death, or disease. Fearing God is the beginning of wisdom. You make wise decisions when you fear God instead of despots, dictators, and desperate bosses. One of the first instances we see of people fearing God is in Exodus 1. Pharaoh's wickedness, in his advancement of slavery in Egypt, was to kill all the boy babies. Scripture tells us that the midwives delivering the babies, "feared God and did not do what Pharaoh commanded them." Thus, we have God's great man of deliverance, Moses. Wisdom in God brings us more and more joy. As bad as a pandemic is, or may one day be, it will surely turn out to be to God's glory. God takes bad things and turns them into His good.

In difficult times people begin to look at mortality, some for the first time. Many discover what we Christ-followers know: Jesus is the only answer. As we run toward the fire, we must be equipped. Prayer is the uniform of the day. You and I should be "prayed up" in order to rush to the rescue. *Prayed up* is a term for being equipped prayerfully for spiritual battle, before you ever get to the battle. Being prayed up means meeting with God, preferably on bended knee, and crying out to Him for strength and guidance. Pray for this world, and pray for your own neighborhood. Pray asking God where He wants you in this battle. For many, He wants you absolutely on your knees. For others, He wants you on the front lines in ministry.

We must have the mind of Christ. Instead of siding with social media woes, thank God for the opportunity to love and minister to people. Christians neither have time to complain, nor to resort to the senseless or irrational. It will squelch your joy quicker than zig-zag lightning to go from talking with God about your problems, to allowing your emotions to be rocked by the 6 o'clock news. Quit spreading propaganda you don't know to be true. Don't just love people, but love them in Jesus' name. Offer them the real light: Jesus saves!

Have you experienced the phenomenon of applying Scripture to your life? It really works. In difficult days people gravitate to Philippians 4:13. Recently someone posted on social media that their week had been tough and, so, *"I can do all things through Christ who strengthens me."* Many people have shown it to me tattooed on their skin. I went to see and help a brother not too long ago who is going through some tough times and, as I was leaving him, he said, "But you know Pastor, I can do all things through Christ who strengthens me!" It's wonderful that it's everywhere, and it's encouraging. But are you sure you understand exactly what Paul meant? Joy is found in knowing exactly what 4:13 means.

We assume that we can just experience God in a personal relationship with Christ without having to know doctrine, but that's impossible. You cannot experience God without knowing who He is, what He has done, and who you are in relation to Him. These things are found in His Holy Word. If we truly love people who are far from God...

➲ People that you meet and greet everyday
➲ People of a different color
➲ People with a different world view
➲ People deemed "out there"
➲ People with a different political view
➲ People that voted differently than you
➲ People that believe faith is believing anything
➲ People who are messed up in their thinking about God
➲ People that don't go to church
➲ People who are sinful in their practices
➲ People...

...if you love them, I mean really love them, you will preach, teach, and live a life through a very specific doctrine, a very defined redemption, and a very specific, precise, and definitive God. Joy is something you receive not from things, but from God. When you give away love and peace, you will understand joy.

The modern-day church has settled for contemporary models to reach people to join the church, and to be successful. It's like the gathering of an eighth-grade student council meeting. The leader says, "Hey, I called this meeting today to see how we can help God and how to make Him more popular!" The vice-president for junior high student affairs pipes up and says, "I know where we can print some cheap fliers and advertise our event!" Another council member says, "We can choose some cool, Top 40 music. That will get the students fired up." And the pimple-faced, high achievers dole out more of their misguided adolescent advice. Substitute the church as the subject of one of these meetings, and you have the same thing that happens in a modern-day church staff meeting.

I saw this advertised on social media:

A movement for Young Adults, aged 18-28. Come and experience community and worship specially designed for you! There's nothing else like it around!

What's wrong with this advertisement? Worship is not designed for us, but for God. God defines what worship He wants. Also, look at their comparison to the competition. The thinking is that if we make our church better, people will come here instead of going there. It's heretic, pathetic, and anti-Gospel.

Is Israel not lesson enough for us? Every time they thought God needed help, they were defeated. We must preach the Gospel message the same way to everyone. We don't need to use a crowbar to lift the tops off of people's

146

dead lives. When we preach the Gospel, our God will blow the tops off of our white-washed tombstones and old bones will come alive again! Is the modern-day church looking to gain joy from the success of their methodology? Sadly, yes.

The Apostle Paul is still in prison as we get close to the end of this letter to the Philippians. I remind you of that because we tend to forget his struggle. Paul isn't sitting under a Middle Eastern fig tree, eating figs and writing in his little journal. He's in a Roman jail. It's dirty, not well-lit, and it stinks. The scene is not like the modern-day penitentiary where there is a cot, three meals, and recreation time. It's definitely nothing like the white-collar reform camps with their tennis courts and other luxuries. Paul is chained to a Roman guard at all times. It was one of those situations where, if your friends from the outside don't come bribe and sweet talk the guards into delivering food to you, then you don't eat. All incarcerated prisoners were at the mercy of family and friends. Paul is in Rome. Not in Philippi, Colossae, or the region of Galatia. Not even in Ephesus. His friends are many, but they are scattered. It wasn't an easy thing for them to get to the jailhouse, much less to take up an offering for food. Here is how it unfolds:

> *I rejoiced in the Lord greatly that now at length you have revived your concern for me. You were indeed concerned for me, but you had no opportunity. Not that I am speaking of being in need, for I have learned in whatever situation I am to be content. I know how to be brought low, and I know how to abound. In any and every circumstance, I have learned the secret of facing plenty and hunger, abundance and need. **I can do all things through him who strengthens me.** -Philippians 4:10-13*

Although the word joy doesn't appear in these few verses, the word, "rejoice" does. In it, you can feel Paul's upbeat attitude of hope and inspiration for the reader. There are at least three takeaways from this passage of Scripture that show us how to grow and mature in Christ in joy. Instead of adding to our possessions in attempt to bring us joy, we need to deal with contentment, circumstances, and dying to ourselves and our concerns. As much as we desire for these last words of Philippians 4 to be about pumping us up, to succeed in any and every circumstance, that's not what they are about. Instead, it's about learning real joy in living this life.

1. Learning to be Content

Contentment means to be satisfied with what you have. Have you mastered that yet? Are you a hoarder? Is your closet full of clothes you will never wear, or never wear again? In all probability, Paul didn't have a change of clothes while in prison, nor was he concerned about fashion. He didn't have a favorite ball team. He wasn't looking to have the new model Ford Bronco and post pictures of it on the Internet. I doubt he had a bank account or a line of credit. If you asked him, he would have responded with a genuine smile on his face, "I'm happy right here." And he meant it. How do you get to that point? How do you learn to be content with what you have?

We often get side-tracked in Christian living when it comes to learning something new. For some reason, many Christians have the disposition that they have arrived at something, rather than making preparations for getting to something great. Sometimes outsiders, the unregenerate, think that when you are a Christian you must have superhero power that keeps you from sinning anymore; that you automatically have faith as fast as a locomotive and strong as superman, to resist evil. We don't. Discipleship, or growing close to God, is like a student sitting under a teacher. Martin Lloyd-Jones said, "We must train ourselves to hate sin." Joy and satisfaction in what you already have, and where you are, is not going to be automatic. You have to *learn* to be content, as Paul says. How do you learn?

➲ **Train yourself to go without** – Fasting is a great spiritual discipline for reminding your body that five meals a day at a buffet is not normal. Skipping a meal to pray is a good thing. I think back to the first time I saw the great flick, *Rocky*. He gets up before the sun comes up to train for his first fight against Apollo Creed. To get quick energy, in order to hit the training hard, he guzzles down four or five raw eggs he has cracked into a glass. Gross! At 14 years old, I thought, "I will never be a good athlete. I can't do that!" The instant protein, though, was exactly what his body needed. Discipline and correct training are essential in the Christian life, but here the result is not instant. There are things you may not want to do, but which have incredible payoffs in the end. Joy is not some fleeting emotion you have to grab onto when it passes by. Train yourself for joy!

➲ **Regularly give stuff away** – Clean out your closet. Give to Goodwill. Give to the Children's Hospital. Donate to a homeless ministry. Participate in ministries that focus on others rather than on yourself. The feeling of "that's mine" needs to be kicked out of your life if you want joy. Truly it is better to give than to receive, but to have that satisfaction and joy you must train yourself to give things

149

away, and to give away your money. How do I know this works, or is the right thing to do? Because it hurts me even to write it, and to think about giving my stuff away. It shows us how really selfish we are when we want to keep things just to keep them. Things do not define you— keep telling yourself that. The Puritans practiced something they called *recollection* before they prayed. It was essentially talking to yourself about yourself. It positioned them to be honest with themselves about who they were. You have to also be honest with yourself about what you have. Things will not bring you joy.

➲ **Window Shop** – What in the world do I mean? It's okay to look at new cars and new houses and new boats and new shoes and new jewelry and say, "That is beautiful!" It's great to appreciate. Appreciate, even more, God's wonderful and beautiful creation. I find it freeing to thank God that others have things they have earned or have been given. Coveting what others have, and being selfish about what you don't have, will wreck your world and keep you from godly joy. Pointing out and appreciating possessions that others have, while thanking God for where you are and what you have, is training to be content. It's sin to think you should have everything you like. Thank God for what He has blessed you with, then smile because you have just grown up a little bit more in Him.

➲ **Always be Thankful** – Always be thankful for what God has given you. We may think we should have more but, from the looks of it, there isn't anyone in my congregation who has missed a meal. Everyone looks pretty satisfied to me each weekend. As I get older, it may be the one thing I am more and more aware of: thankfulness. I hate to say it, but I notice when others don't thank me. I don't mean I am angry at their ingratitude. For sure I've missed expressing thanks to others at times. What I mean is, as our world progresses in the belief that more and more *stuff* makes us happy, I also see a corresponding decrease in gratitude. Gratefulness to God is an instant joy builder.

2. Living in all Circumstances

Is there a better scenario to illustrate Philippians 4:10-13 than the COVID-19 crisis we have been through? When you meet Jesus, it's the advancement of God in your life, not circumstances, that dictate your life. Paul covered the whole spectrum: *"I've had a lot, and I've had nothing. I have been rich and I have been poor. It doesn't matter. The only thing that matters is Christ."* Let me say it clearly and without ambiguity— if churches close their doors because of a virus or any other health issue, it isn't because God told them to. It is because the state, or government, pressured them into it. If we are going to quit, to shutter the meetings and stop gathering together, and if we are going to quiver and kowtow to epidemics and pandemics, then what in the world are we going to do in the future of other tragedies sure to come? What are we going to do when the real trouble comes? There are new philosophies and ideologies on the horizon that seek to wipe out Christianity in America.

What are we going to do when martial law prevents us from attending regular worship on the weekend?

Think of our brothers and sisters in Christ currently living in Iran, Myanmar, and China, for example. They dodge arrest and prison on a regular basis because they are barred from meeting as a church, but they do it anyway. They are true risk-takers for God. Here, meanwhile, we have the freedom to meet and we say we believe our God is all-powerful and almighty and He is able to heal us or keep us from harm and sickness. Yet we don't trust Him? We refuse to meet with Him in something called church? Here are some prophetic words: God will not put up with that for very long.

Am I saying that we should voluntarily expose ourselves to viruses and other life-threatening fears? Maybe. As believers we have to learn to live in all circumstances. Jesus gave His life for us. When is the last time you risked your life for Him? We need to pray and lead our families in what is safe for us and them, of course. But as things get worse— and they will— will you continually decide to keep living to self, rather than dying to your own desires?

I'm not saying we are being cold and callous toward disease and the coming changes in the world structure. But if we shared and preached the Gospel with the same clarity that we stressed wearing a mask during the Coronavirus pandemic, then many more would be saved in Christ. I guarantee it. We became experts in disinfecting the worship center, while we were pathetic in preaching the washing away of our sins. The local church was better versed in cleaning the door handles and improving air pollution than they were in dealing with polluted souls.

Recently I listened to podcasts of pastors talking about virus precautions, hashing and rehashing the need to display hand sanitizer and washing of hands, but I rarely heard them lead in prayer. COVID-19 has been terrible, but the sin virus in people is far worse. It kills the soul. Who is going to stand up and blow the shofar? Who is going to say, "Who is this enemy that defies the living God?" Who is going to say to the giant, "You come at me sickness and chaos, and try to get me to fear you, but I come at you in the name of the God of angel armies!" How do you and I live in circumstances like these and others to come? Here's how I live and seek joy in my life each day:

➲ **Pray the Psalms** – Read the Psalms every day. With diligence you can read several a day and, by the end of the year, you will have read through the Psalms at least seven times. They are your lifeline to encouragement. The Psalms describe the character and movement of God. Nothing speaks to me like the Psalms do. With them I worship, I reflect, and I meditate on His greatness. Whatever the world throws at you, open up the Psalms and your heart will be calmed. Study them, ponder them, and pray them. If you do, your life will change. I promise.

➲ **Ride the highs and lows** – Paul says he's been up and down. His life has had its highs and lows. It's the same with you and me. Not long ago I was checking out of the grocery store, inserting my card and pressing my PIN, and I heard the conversation of the lady behind me in line. The cashier was making small talk with the young man bagging my groceries about the rising concerns of COVID-19, and the lady behind me was talking on her mobile phone with her earbuds in her ears (I hate that). I overheard her say, nonchalantly, "Well, these are stressful times." Guess what?

All times are stressful. Life is full of highs and lows. When the high ones come, try to remember your God because you will definitely cry out to Him in the lows. The highs and lows are like waves. Job says it like this: *"He alone spreads out the heavens, And treads on the waves of the sea."* Jesus was asleep when the disciples were frightened by the waves, but when they awoke Him He calmed the sea. When the high tides of devastation are too tumultuous in our lives, remember Him. When the low tides of despair invade our lives, remember Him. What should you do? Remember God.

⮑ **Get Ready for "any" and "all"** – This is important. I think Paul says any and all because we shouldn't be surprised by the next attack of the enemy. Habitually the strategy of Satan is called, "Rock-a-bye Baby." He lulls us to sleep. We long to reach normal in an abnormal world. We want things to be calm, peaceful and blissful. And all the while we commit our little sins, thinking nothing of them. They build, and then the collapse comes. The Christian life should be one of readiness, preparedness. Jesus tells the parable of the virgins, five who were prepared for the groom, and five who weren't. The five who played around got left behind. They weren't ready for any or all. You must be prepared.

3. Dying to all Concerns

It alarms me as pastor, and as a spiritual leader of my community and my church, when I see someone on social media posting their anxieties over the tragedies in the world, and not clinging to the promises of God. I get concerned about the spiritual health of people who are stressed out to the point of depression over a political party or candidate, and don't put prayer first and live the transformed life of Christ. When we fear a virus that can only kill our bodies, and we are not at all concerned about the one that can kill our souls, I wonder about our commitment to God. I am concerned about a neighborhood, city, nation, world that will bow down to the whims of a philosophy but won't bow down to the Savior who suffered and died to take away our sin. I am very concerned when the church looks to conform to society for the sake of unity and harmony, then covers it up with excuses rather than standing tall for *Jesus first*. I am dismayed over the Christian who seeks first to save their own hide rather than to put their life on the line for Christ. People are going to die and go to hell tomorrow because somewhere— somewhere in these United States— someone will have stayed home because church was canceled today. Tomorrow they will meet their Maker, and they weren't ready.

Two thousand years ago there was both an epidemic and a pandemic. The epidemic was leprosy. Leprosy is a disease that affects the nervous system and, if left untreated, the bacterial infection will cause fingers and limbs to rot off and will cause blindness, among other terrible physical infirmities. If you had this terrible disease in Year One A.D., you were definitely quarantined and you didn't get out. There was no vaccine coming anytime soon. You lived in a commune with other lepers, awaiting a gruesome death.

At the same time there was a pandemic, and it still exists. There is no medicinal cure, no sanitization from it, and all have it. Everyone is infected. It's called sin. We are sinners, and Jesus came to die for our pandemic— and He did die for it. Yet, people still live as if this pandemic doesn't

155

exist. It's real, but most prefer to seek happiness by trying to live longer, freer, and richer. How do we respond to epidemics and pandemics? The answer is Philippians 4:13. If there ever was a time for you to stand up for God, gird your trust, ignore the partisan crowd, and shout, "I can do all things through Christ who gives me strength," it's now. What does He give us strength for? For the joy in living.

Jesus was passing through a region between Samaria and Galilee and up ahead, on a ridge, there was an eerie looking landscape. It must have looked like a scene out of a zombie TV show. Moving closer, any normal person would have been freaked out. It would have caught anyone off guard. There, now close at hand, were ten people standing side by side. One has to wonder if they were dressed in white robes, swaying in the wind, to create this frightening scene. As He walked a few feet closer, He could see their skin. It was a horrific sight. Lepers! He could smell them a hundred yards away. They cried out to the Lord, *"Jesus, Master, have mercy on us."* The Lord said, *"Go show yourself to the priest,"* and the Scriptures tell us as they went, they were healed. Next, one of them turned around, remembering the Lord, and as he fell on his face to Jesus, and he said, *"thank you."* Jesus, sardonic maybe, but serious nonetheless, said, *"Weren't there ten of you? Where are the other nine?"* Jesus then tells him, *"Get up, your faith has made you well."*

Fear is coming to this world. For those without eyes to see and ears to hear the Master, it will be awful. Joy will be the last thing on the minds of those without Christ. Pain is seeking you out these days. We've seen good times and we've seen bad. We've had money and there have been times we were without. Have you learned yet to trust Jesus in all things? In **all things**? Paul doesn't say "I can do the good things that are good for me that I know are tough... through Christ who strengthens me." No, he says *all things*. He knows there are some things that we don't understand why we even go through them. But God is faithful. He always has been and always will be. True joy comes in knowing the Master by faith. Thank Him today for dying on the Cross for you, and bow to Him, then you will find joy in the middle of your hurts, circumstances, and concerns.

Chapter 11 – **JOY123** Study Guide:

J1 It is very important to note Paul's words, "I rejoice *in the Lord*." If you remove them then his words about suffering, and his thanks to them for caring, don't mean much. Notice Paul's constant referral, devotion, and deferment to God and God's purpose in **JESUS**. The pursuit of joy can quickly go south when we go selfish. Grammatically speaking, our joy has to have an object other than ourselves. Joy must be found "in Christ." Paul rejoices in Christ, and therefore he can do all things through Christ. Worship Him today by serving Him. Serving Him sometimes means doing good stuff in His name. What can you do today to know He is working in you and strengthening you?

_____
_____
_____
_____
_____
_____
_____
_____
_____

02 Ezra is this little Old Testament book about the rebuilding of the Temple of God after God's people were exiled and taken captive by the Babylonians. The original Temple had been destroyed, and Ezra, a priest and scribe, was commissioned to rebuild it. There are at least four verses where the writer tells us about the joy of [OTHERS] the people as they were rebuilding, and after they finished, and how the joy had returned following their obedience in worshipping Him. Read Ezra 6 and see if you can experience the "joy" with them because they had once again had a place to worship God. Write in a few sentences what it means to you to go to church:

_____

_____

_____

_____

_____

_____

_____

_____

Y3 If YOU had Philippians 4:13 tattooed on your heart (maybe you do), then what would (does) it mean? What things would you do, or would you want to do, for the Lord? Take a few minutes to dream about great spiritual things to take place in your life. Why do you live for Him? What do you want to be remembered for when it comes to serving God?

_____

_____

_____

_____

_____

_____

Chapter 12

The Supplier

I have had the great privilege of proclaiming the Gospel in prisons all over my state. I have walked through those dank restraining iron bar doors that utter "you are trapped," and I immediately began to feel the isolation, separation, and despair that so many live while in a penitentiary. If you are going to visit someone in prison, or going in to minister in the name of the Lord Jesus, you can't take anything in with you— except maybe a Bible. Doors begin closing electronically behind you as you walk further into the steel, concrete, and barbed wire structure. If you ever watched the 1960's comedy show *Get Smart,* with its succession of opening and closing steel doors, it's eerily similar.

One does not know what to expect inside the walls of a prison and you will unconsciously practice social distancing, if you know what I mean. It's frightening not knowing how you will be received. I've rubbed elbows with many murderers and high-profile criminals. That's a scary thing. Most of the time, though, I've been met with kind incarcerated gentlemen who were excited we were there. Only a very few times did I feel uncomfortable enough to try to keep a guard in my sight in case of the worst. Of course, usually in a prison church service setting the guard is all the way at the other side of the room, so not a lot of good that would have done me. The key is to settle down to trust that God is going to protect you. I would venture to say that most of us have never been deep inside a prison, and particularly not a Middle Eastern one. But this is where the Apostle Paul is chronicling from as we finish up the great book of Philippians.

Although the book of Philippians is about joy, the setting is the antithesis of this great biblical fruit. We have thus far found literal, literature-based spiritual jewels to apply to our lives in these chapters. Amazingly, the final verses apply to us in exactly the place we find ourselves socially in the world today. God leads us to the answer and to the soothing assuredness that He is with us— His people, the church.

Joy in prison is an irony. Paul is chained to a guard 24/7 but he's clear on his mission. As he stated in chapter 1, *"For to me, to live is Christ, to die is gain."* In chapter 2 he tells us to have the mind of Christ, while telling us that one day every knee will bow before Him— conservative or liberal or moderate— every knee; rich, poor, or middle class— every knee; college educated, major league superstar, NFL player, Wall Street executive, Washington pundit, Academy Award winner, or cave dweller—every knee; American, Russian, Chinese, or Latino— every knee. It is *every* knee that will one day bow before King Jesus. In chapter 3, he encourages us to keep running the race of life, saying, *"I forget what is behind and press on to the goal, which is upwards, which is Christ Jesus."* In the last chapter, we talked about verse 13 of chapter 4, *"I can do all things through Christ, who strengthens me."* A better translation from the Greek is "In all things, I have strength from the One strengthening me." Now, let's start from that sweet verse 13:

> *I can do all things through him who strengthens me. Yet it was kind of you to share my trouble. And you Philippians yourselves know that in the beginning of*

the gospel, when I left Macedonia, no church entered into partnership with me in giving and receiving, except you only. Even in Thessalonica you sent me help for my needs once and again. Not that I seek the gift, <u>but I seek the fruit that increases to your credit</u>. I have received full payment, and more. I am well supplied, having received from Epaphroditus the gifts you sent, a fragrant offering, a sacrifice acceptable and pleasing to God. <u>And my God will supply every need of yours according to his riches in glory in Christ Jesus</u>. —Philippians 4:13-19*

This church at Philippi would be about ten years old by this time. A decade-old church is usually well established. Leaders will have been developed and ministry organized. Paul is chained and restricted, but he is still conducting God's business. He is still preaching, teaching, encouraging, and running the ministry. This is nuts, because most of us would have called it quits long ago if in prison, in Paul's situation. But the obstacles became opportunity for Paul. Here's what it teaches us:

1. Obstacles become Opportunity for us

God allows health and spiritual pandemics for a purpose. God is not caught off guard today by the Coronavirus of 2020-21, or by any other health crisis. Trials in our lives serve as launching pads for our own growth in faith and occasion to love others. Paul says "thank you" numerous times in chapter 4. He doesn't necessarily use the exact words but he says, "I have joy because you remembered me and gave to me," "It was kind for you to share," and "No one else gave but you." These are all Paul's way of saying thanks, and look at the epic words he

161

produced that have been so massive to our faith in Christ: "I can do all things through Christ who strengthens me."

I guarantee you the headlines in hell in the spring of 2020 were, "COVID-19 hits Planet Earth, Churches are done for!" But the true believer knows we have been preparing for this and worse. The church is not a building, but the people. Incredible, but as I am writing this, our church is in the middle of constructing our first building. And, for us, it is a reminder that we don't consist of a group of people who gather in a concrete and wood structure just to tell each other, for one hour a week, it's going to be okay. That is not us at all.

Paul says, "I appreciate you sharing your troubles with me," and we should follow his lead during times of difficulty and trouble among fellow believers. As Christians, it's in our DNA to show love, to minister to, and to set the example of kindness. But more than that, Philippians is directing us to use the trouble— not to cry or sulk or panic or worry or fear— but to treat every obstacle as a springboard to loving others. It is our Christian duty to bring joy in a hurting world.

Look at challenges, such as a quarantine, in a positive way. How do you minister to people in the name of the Lord Jesus Christ without being able to meet with them or talk with them? It's tricky, because our normal touchy-feely Christian selves don't hardly know how to minister without patting people on the back or hugging the blues out of someone in Jesus' name. Here's some help:

> ⮕ **Pray for the harvest** – If there is one thing I am confident will come out of difficult times, it is this: God always leads us out of despair into revival. Tough times are simply disguised opportunities for you to take a stand of trust in God, showing your belief in Him. King David is talking about difficult times in Psalm 69, and

gives us the answer in verse 29: "You who seek God, let your hearts revive." Pray for revival in your heart.

⮑ **Prepare for the harvest** – What is the basis of Philippians 4? Giving. The spiritual obstacle automatically generated by our hardships is the ability to give. We are takers by nature. But when you have little, it's your greatest opportunity for massive spiritual gains. Paul makes a point of saying, 'everybody forgot me, but not you Philippians. You are the only ones.' Look at this present-day society we live in and you will see that the majority of people are looking for cash bonuses and government handouts. As Christians, we don't go with the flow, but are supposed to go the opposite direction. We run toward the problem!

How many of you have a little ICHTHUS tattoo, or bumper sticker on your car? Notice that the little fish that symbolizes *Christian* is always swimming against the grain. In reality, we don't need more tattoos of Jesus on our sleeves, but we need His Word tattooed on our hearts! Prepare by giving. Giving what? Everything.

⮑ **Preach the harvest** – If you can't meet with someone and tell them about how God is blessing your life, then write them a letter or send them an email. Use your time wisely, and use technology greatly. Text them, inbox them, or just pick up the phone and dial their number. The days are growing shorter, time is flying by quickly. If you can't bring them to church, talk to them about the Lord. Ask a simple question that will cut through all of the junk: How is your relationship with God?

2. Faith is mobilized into Fruit for us

I eat a lot of fruit. I eat at least one piece, if not two to three pieces, of fruit each day. I like chocolate better. I like ice cream a whole lot better. I like ice cream with chocolate on it best of all. But a banana split is not going to give me the physical strength I will need as I get older. My body craves the right kind of energy, not just anything sitting in my stomach. In the same way, we need right faith— not just faith in anything or anybody. It is easy to miss, though it may be the entire purpose of this passage of Scripture when Paul says, "I appreciate the gift." It may have been money, it may have been food, it may have been a blanket— it was probably all of the above. But, regardless, here's the core of how he felt: "*Not that I seek the gift, but I seek the fruit that increases to your credit.*" Here are our own normal responses to receiving gifts:

- ➲ We write a thank you note
- ➲ We give a verbal "thank you"
- ➲ We are spoiled and unappreciative and don't do or say anything
- ➲ We snatch up that gift card, go out immediately and spend it on ourselves
- ➲ We re-gift!

Paul says *What you gave, I didn't ask for*, and really the point of whether or not he needed it is irrelevant. Rather, Paul looks forward to what the giving will produce. That's unselfishness, and that is true faith and love. Quit stacking up God's blessings and start using them to bless others. Then you will be blessed more than you can stand.

Giving is a difficult subject at any time in our selfish world but giving during poor times, jobless times, or

164

personal economic disaster times truly doesn't make sense to most people. Why? Because our eyes are still on ourselves and not on the fruit our giving will produce down the line.

Paul is saying, in effect: I'm not going to spend the money on me, it's for the ministry. It's for others. It's so we can start more churches and more people can turn to Christ as the answer in their difficult, dead-end lives. It's for fruit! Something good is going to come from your giving, Paul says. You can't see it, or maybe you don't understand it, but giving your time praying, or giving your time serving, or giving your money, or giving your gift— truly giving to God's vision— is your faith being mobilized to bring about fruit.

> *Abide in me, and I in you. As the branch cannot bear fruit by itself, unless it abides in the vine, neither can you, unless you abide in me. I am the vine; you are the branches. Whoever abides in me and I in him, he it is that bears much fruit, for apart from me you can do nothing.* *-John 15:4,5*

I've noticed something about the fruit I buy. If I don't eat it, it spoils. I bought green bananas the other day, but it didn't matter. After a week, they were brown and spotted and ugly. If you don't eat an apple, that usually great bite turns into a mealy mess. Strawberries (my favorite) will draw up and turn sour. Unless your faith in God is tested regularly, how do you know you have digested His truth? The Psalmist says, "Taste and see that the Lord is good." Jesus says, you have to be pruned, cut back, cut up, to grow to more fruit. Fruit is given and fruit is used to produce more fruit. It's the picture of the church. God gives us the fruit, but if that fruit isn't used to nourish others, He takes it away.

3. Supply comes from God's Stash for us

When the hitches and complications of life come our way, what do we want? We want comfort. Sometimes that comfort comes by cash or a hot meal, but it all boils down to someone else helping us because we can't help ourselves so readily. We want someone who cares to help us. As we read the Word of God and survey the problems of the world today, and ponder whatever else is going to come our way in our lifetime, we find that God supplies our needs and He will give us our wants— *as long as it's what He wants.*

You see, He gives to us and supplies us with the thing we really long for: He gives us the comfort of His presence. It's all you need, and it's what you really want. Paul modeled it for us. God will give you cash— the ability to cash in your worries and fear for the real currency, which is trusting in Him. He will give you a party— a party of friends at church to face life's trials with. He will give you promotion after promotion— to promote the Gospel message to lost friends and acquaintances. He will give you gold— to lead those struggling, those without the Lord, to the streets of gold.

True churches are like the Philippian church in this way. We share and trust God in difficult times, and we know He will give us what we need. While news reporters, politicians, sages, and preachers are telling you what to do in the hardship days, let me tell you the absolute best thing you can do: take Philippians 4:19 and write it out, post it on your refrigerator, on your mirror, use it as a bookmark. Whatever you do, remember it, because days could get tough for you. We are apt to believe the enemy and that we should fear even the reaper, but don't. God will give His people everything they need. Paul puts it like this: "*And my God will supply every need of yours according to his riches in glory in Christ Jesus.*" My friends, that and only that, is real joy.

Chapter 12 – **JOY123** Study Guide:

01   Bernard of Clairvaux, the Benedictine monk of nine hundred years ago, delightfully said that the name of **JESUS** is "honey in the mouth, melody in the ear, and joy in the heart." Maybe he was on to something. Just speaking the name of **JESUS** brings joy. How often do you say the name **JESUS** out loud? How often do you silently call upon Him by name? Add the sweet, beautiful name of **JESUS** to your conversations and watch as joy is more and more evident.

02   Have you missed the opportunity to be a supplier of God's goodness and gifts to **OTHERS**? Often we miss out on giving because we forget. We have good intentions of helping **OTHERS**, but we push them aside for a more convenient moment or for a time when we have an overabundance of resources. Here's the answer: Plan to give. Write out a schedule of giving. It could take place over a course of a week, a month, or a year or two. It's very satisfying to plan to give, and then to execute the plan. Try it.

_____

_____

_____

_____

_____

_____

_____

_____

_____

_____

Y3 There is power in a blessing. As the Apostle Paul completes the great letter to the Romans, in the second to the last chapter he pronounces this blessing on **YOU** and me: *"May the God of hope fill you with all joy and peace in believing, so that by the power of the Holy Spirit you may abound in hope"* (Romans 15:13). Through it all, remember, God is the one who supplies your joy. He gives **YOU** joy so that **YOU** will continue to grow as you hope in Christ. Write a prayer of hope here, and pray it, the by-product will be joy!

_____

_____

_____

_____

_____

_____

_____

_____

_____

_____

_____

_____

_____

_____

_____

_____

_____

Epilogue

One Sunday morning during church, the pastor made a passionate plea for workers for the children's ministry. Sandy was a teenager in the youth department and in between texting her girlfriends sitting behind her and giggling, she heard the pastor's appeal. She loved children, so she volunteered to help out in the toddler department. This adventure would be her first in teaching, and she was nervous.

Having just got her driver's license, Sandy loved to hang out with her friends at church, and was eager to know more of God. Just ten months before, she knew the Holy Spirit was speaking to her heart and had made the decision to give her life to Christ. But like many of her adolescent friends, the boldness to serve Jesus in this selfish world was yet unrealized or undeveloped.

On her first Sunday, Sandy was introduced to the smiling three- and four-year-olds by their teacher, Mrs. Maytrude White. Mother Maytrude had been teaching children for over fifty years. She was a sweet, gray-haired soul with a very soft granny voice. Developmental psychology tells us we listen closely to soft voices.

"Boys and girls," Mrs. White said gently, "this is Miss Sandy, our new assistant teacher. She is going to be helping out every Sunday in our class. Please welcome her."

Some of the children clapped, most just smiled and waved. Mrs. White was in her second week of a lively study called *The Fruit of the Spirit*. The week before, she had shared and taught about love. This week the subject was joy.

Here's what that sweet, gentle soul shared with the children:

"When Jesus died on the Cross for our sins, He won! We are winners with Him. All of God's children get to share in His victory by dying for our sin."

The children were trying to be attentive, fidgeting a little, and some of them interrupted by raising their hands. Sandy held her finger up to her lips in attempt to help Mrs. White maintain order.

Little Henry politely raised his hand and asked, "But Mrs. White, what about the children in China?"

She smiled and said, "Yes, Jesus died for them too!"

Then Anna's hand shot up and Mrs. White asked, "Yes, Anna, do you have a question?"

Anna said, "Yes ma'am. What does it mean when you say Jesus died for my sins?"

It's a great question isn't it? Mrs. White took a deep breath and responded, "Children, as you grow up you will find that you will have to make more and more decisions, and sometimes it will be difficult. Your mom and dad may not be around, and God doesn't want you to ever be alone. He wants you to know He loves you. But the problem is we sin, and sin means we do bad things, we choose to do the wrong thing instead of the good things of God. Your sin and my sin makes us separated from God. It put us in jail where we can't be close to God. When Jesus died on the Cross... He killed that sin, and now we are free!"

Anna smiled. She seemed to get it.

As Mrs. White was wrapping up the lesson, she asked Sandy if she had anything to add. Sandy wasn't used to being put on the spot. She thought for a moment and remembered the Wednesday night youth meeting a few weeks ago. The sermon was on how to have joy in your life.

170

Sandy recalled her student pastor saying, "Okay guys, remember it like this: JOY-123...Jesus first, others second, you third...that's how to have real joy!"

She proudly repeated that same jubilant sounding jingle to the toddlers, "JOY-123" she said.

"Say it with me... JOY-123," and all the kids joined in with Sandy. She continued, "It means put Jesus first, others second, and yourself third!"

JOY-123 is a fantastic little axiom and proverb to remember how to have joy. Short, pithy abbreviations help us learn. What does it mean? It's the same thing Mrs. White taught her children that day. But what was Mrs. White's lesson? Don't miss it. Every smart, Gospel-loving, and biblical children's teacher presents the Good News of Christ each week as plainly and as easy to understand as possible. The Gospel message is very clear, according to the Apostle Paul in 1 Corinthians 15. Simple, yet very deep: *Jesus died, was buried, and then rose again.*

Mrs. White smiled. she was proud of her new assistant teacher for adding the perfect summary to finish her lesson on joy. The class then sang a closing song and prayed, then the parents began coming by and collecting their children to go home. Sandy gathered her things, was thanked by Mrs. White, and she headed out the door for Sunday lunch with her family.

After church, little Anna held her mom's hand as they walked across the parking lot to their mini-van.

"Mommy, mommy, that's Miss Sandy!" she exclaimed as she spied Sandy getting into her car.

Sandy turned and waved, hearing the little girl's voice. Anna's mom spoke up and introduced herself, and thanked Sandy for helping with her daughter's class. Anna was proud.

"Anna, did you tell your mom what you learned today?" Sandy asked.

The shy little four-year-old said, "Mommy, we learned JOY-123."

"What does that mean honey?" Anna's mom asked.

Anna answered, in her child's manner, "Jesus won, Others too, and Me free."

Anna understood the deep, deep truth, whereas many, many have turned away from the joy of life that comes from the Savior. Jesus said, "Truly, I say to you, whoever does not receive the kingdom of God like a child shall not enter it."

Joy is discovering Jesus is the winner, and the world continues to turn until He comes back for those who bow their knee to the King in repentance of sin. Yes, you too...and when you do, you are free. It's a great 1-2-3.

Joy should be on your mind, on your heart, and in your words and attitude every day. He won it at the Cross...for you too...and when you turn from your sins to Him, you are free.

About the Author

Greg Dowey is the Founding Pastor at Fresh Church in Chapin, South Carolina. Pastor Greg is passionate about expository preaching, short-term missionary work, and the body of Christ – the church. He is the author of two previous titles, *Eight: The Book About Just One Chapter* and *The Great Go Mission*, both published in 2020.

Pastor Greg holds a Doctor of Ministry (DMIN) from North Greenville University. He and his wife Missie run Simple Ministries, a mission to supply Bibles and preach the Gospel around the globe. They have one son, Jack, who is working on a master's degree from the University of Southern California.

Visit Pastor Greg's website at gddowey.com.

Other Books by GD Dowey

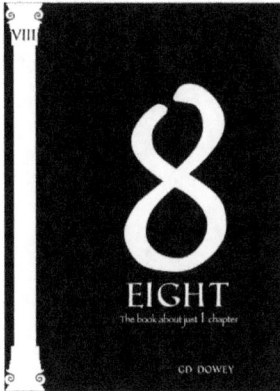

Eight: The Book About Just One Chapter

ISBN 978-1-7359876-0-6

A study of Romans 8, perhaps the greatest chapter in the Bible. Dr. Dowey reminds us of the freedom we have in Jesus Christ and shows us that walking with Jesus is a new beginning and that God is more interested in our transformation as believers than the political and geographical alteration of nations.

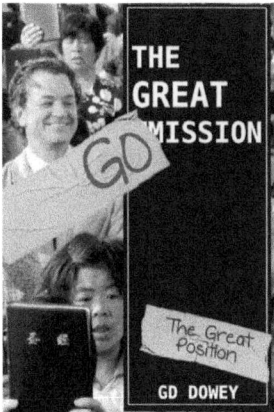

The Great Go Mission

ISBN 978-1-7359876-1-3

In this book, Dr. GD Dowey gives deep personal insight into short-term mission projects and challenges the reader to GO, whether it's across the street or across the globe. He lays a Biblically-based and historical foundation, then follows the changes in missions—both good and bad—and offers recommendations for how to get started and how to GO.

Available in paperback from major online book retailers, and in Kindle e-book edition from Amazon.

9 781735 987620